WORTH

From Saxon S

to

Seaside Town

Ronald Kerridge

and

Michael Standing

Optimus Books, Worthing

First published 2000 by Optimus Books Ltd.
27 Warwick Street, Worthing, West Sussex, BN11 3DQ

ISBN 0 95331324 7

Printed and bound in Great Britain by Biddles Ltd, Guildford, Surrey

CONTENTS

LIST OF MAPS, DRAWINGS AND PHOTOGRAPHS

This Book was inspired by
The Worthing Art Development Publications
and is dedicated to
the pioneering effort of
Worthing's first local historians
Edward Snewin and Henfrey Smail

Acknowledgements

The authors would like to thank the following for their assistance :
Worthing Borough Council for permission to search and use information from the Town Hall archives; Mr. Roger J. Wilson for the use of the Broadwater Manor court books; Mr. Martin Hayes and the staff at Worthing Reference Library; Mr. Richard Childs and the staff at West Sussex Record Office; the late John Norwood, Dr. Sally White and the staff at Worthing Museum and Art Gallery; Mrs Eileen Colwell; Messrs. Robert Elleray, Alan Cowdrey, Ken Jakes, Keith Nethercote-Bryant, Mike Prince, Phil Fry, Chris Bradley, Brian Curtis, Roy Bradford, Mike Lawrence, Ron Evans, Denis Prosser and the late Terry Child.

Acknowledgements for Illustrations

Most of the line drawings were prepared by the authors and other illustrations are from their own archives. The authors are indebted to Worthing Library for figures 24, 26, 28, 29, 30, 31, 33, 34, 37, 38, 39, 49, 50, 53, 56, 57, 58, 60, 63, 64, 65, 66, 67, 68, 69, 75, 76, 77, 79, 81, 82, 83 and 84: Worthing Museum and Art Gallery for figures 32, 48, 51, 52, 55, 59, 70, 71 and 78: Alan Cowdrey for figures 21, 22, 23, 41 and 87 and the West Sussex Record Office for figure 17.

1. EARLY SETTLEMENT

While many excellent books have been written on divergent aspects of Worthing's past history, this book focuses on the factors and constraints that influenced its evolution over the past two millennia. It is the product of 25 years' research, the information having been gleaned from a wide range of sources.

The modern town of Worthing is situated on the fertile coastal plain that extends from Brighton in East Sussex into Hampshire, a distance of over 40 miles [64km], the largest part being within the administrative boundaries of West Sussex.

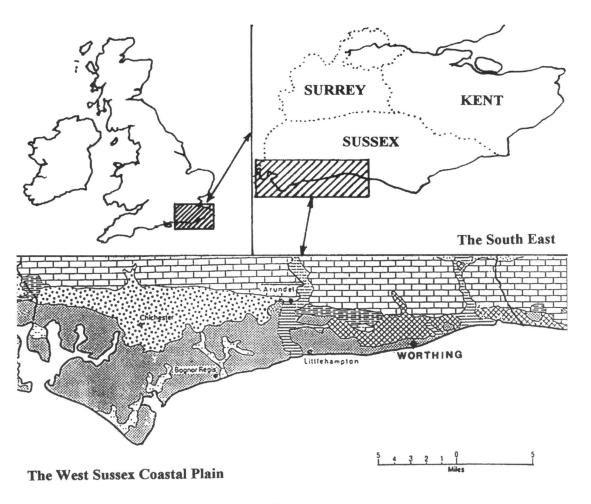

The West Sussex Coastal Plain

Fig. 1 Maps showing location and geology of Worthing area

The relative flatness of the land on which the modern town is sited is the result of events that occurred over five hundred thousand years ago, when great sheets of polar ice advanced and retreated over much of Northern Siberia and North America. It had always been considered unlikely that any of these Pleistocene glaciations resulted in the ice sheets covering South East England, with the major movements in the ice ceasing at the Thames Valley. Recent seismic profiling, however, now suggests the possibility of glacial activity in the English Channel and on the South Downs.[1] With each glacial advance, ocean water froze to become polar ice and with each retreat the polar ice melted to return water to the oceans. As a consequence the sea level fell and rose as the ages came and went, and in the vicinity of Worthing the sea once lapped the southern foot of Highdown. The coastal plain is a remnant of the floor of this sea, bevelled by the slowly encroaching waves, and was ultimately exposed following the final retreat of the water during the last Ice Age.[2]

Men of the Paleolithic or Old Stone Age first arrived in South East England when Britain was still part of the Northern European land mass, during the warmer phases of the glacial period before the last retreat of the ice.[3] The recent discovery and analysis of the 'Boxgrove Man' archaeological site has vastly extended our knowledge of Paleolithic man and his environment. During their intermittent visits these early nomadic hunters lived in the open and survived by hunting and gathering wild plants. Their flint tools were primarily used for obtaining food, and were probably made from flint found on the surface of the ground. Flint tools of this period have been found in the Worthing area and several are on display in Worthing Museum.

At the close of the Ice Age, about ten thousand years, ago changes in climate brought about the collapse of the hunting civilisations of Old Stone Age man. Temperatures rose, glaciers and ice sheets melted and sea levels rose, albeit intermittently, from a level about 100 feet [30m] below the present sea level. During this rise the mouths of the rivers draining southwards across the coastal plain flooded to form estuaries, and the mouths of minor streams like the Teville Stream and Sompting Brook became wide tidal creeks or inlets.[4] According to Dr. Frederick Dixon, a mid-nineteenth-century Worthing geologist, the extent of this broad expanse of brackish water, from which the village of Broadwater possibly took its name,[5] could easily be discerned by its level, the character of the soil, which in some places was mere shingle, and the presence of marine shells of existing species.[6] Modern geological investigations substantiate his statements, as the ground conditions found in the area of the former 'braden waetre'[7] are a very shallow covering of alluvium, over a fine pale grey silty clay. The alluvium found consisted of soft estuarine soils, consistent with an infilled creek, resulting from a change of sea level relative to land in fairly recent geological time.[8]

Exactly when Britain was separated from the continent of Europe remains uncertain, but lithic evidence suggests a date prior to 6000 BC.[9] As the climate improved substantial vegetation reappeared, and by 6000 BC most of South East England was covered by forests of elm, oak, elder and lime. It was not, however, until c. 4300 BC that communities of Neolithic or New Stone Age man first settled in the Worthing area. The impact of these first farmers on the landscape was considerable.[10] With them came a new communal culture in which cattle-raising and food production replaced hunting and gathering. Fundamental to their way of life was a good supply of flint axes and other tools, which were essential for clearing the forests, agricultural purposes and for building shelter.[11]

It appears these farmers soon found the flint obtained from the chalk was far better for tool production than that lying on the surface, and flint mining clearly became an integral part of the activities of these early farming communities. The flint mines at Church Hill (Findon), Blackpatch, Harrow Hill and Cissbury, estimated to have been in existence prior to 3700 BC, are among the earliest in Britain.[12] It has been calculated that at Cissbury Hill, to the north of the modern town of Worthing, there were between 97 to 200 mine shafts. [13] Although Cissbury had less mine shafts than Harrow Hill (160 shafts), it appears it was the first to attract the curiosity of antiquaries,[14] and from the abundance of

Fig. 2 *Yeakell and Gardner's map of c.1780 showing Cissbury and tidal inlet (hatched)*

Fig. 3 *Flint axe, scraper and arrow-head found at Cissbury*

archaeological finds it is evident that it was one of the largest flint-mining areas in this country, second only to those at Grimes Graves in Norfolk. Since the output of flint tools at Cissbury appears to be far in excess of those required for local use, it is now thought that many were distributed to other areas.[15] There is a fine model of a flint mine in Worthing Museum together with many examples of flint tools created from Cissbury's flint-mining activities.

The use of metal, copper and tin at first, and then bronze, marks a significant economic and social change. Following the introduction of copper, many of the larger flint tools were replaced by superior bronze tools. Smaller flint tools, such as scrapers, arrow-heads, awls etc., however continued to be used until some time after 1400 BC.

Most of the visible remains at Cissbury belong to the Iron Age, for in *c*. 350 BC a hill fort was constructed on its summit, enclosing part of the former area of the flint mines.[16] Situated in a central position on the South Downs between the rivers Adur and the Arun it was an elongated oval which enclosed over 60 acres [24.28 hectares]. Its entrances, which still exist today, were on the south and east sides. Despite its vast size there is no positive evidence to show whether or not its interior was ever densely or continuously inhabited during the Iron Age. Traces of Iron Age cultivation in the form of lynchets (raised field boundaries) are, however, recorded in the vicinity of Cissbury.[17] It is a significant relic of Iron Age Britain, and remains a prominent feature of the landscape today. Although research into the post-100 BC Late Iron Age settlement of the coastal plain is still at an early stage a picture is gradually emerging. From the scant evidence found to date it would appear that the infiltration of settlement onto the coastal plain was either due to migration from the overpopulated downland areas, or the declining fertility of the South Downs.[18] The fertile soils of the coastal plain were at last discovered and exploited .

The period of Roman occupation from AD 43 is one of the most distinctive and dynamic episodes in the history of the South East. The evidence of Roman rule is still with us today. Traffic thunders along roads like Stane Street, laid down to spread the movement of the legions from the fortified town of *Noviomagus* (Chichester) to *Londinium* (London), which was the nerve centre of the country and the focal point for communications between province and empire. The archaeological evidence for the Roman period is considerable and traces of settlement like the villas at Bignor and Angmering, portions of which were probably built between AD 70 and 80, substantiate the rapid development and prosperity of Sussex during the early years of the Roman occupation.[19]

The basis of the wealth of the Roman economy was land, and its exploitation by farming to produce sufficient surpluses to support the more sophisticated aspects of Roman life.[20] A considerable amount of capital was invested into grain production to satisfy not only the increase in population but also an export market.[21] While there has been a considerable amount of time and resources spent on the study of villas, given its importance there has been relatively little detailed examination of land use and field systems.[22] This is probably because the combination of centuries of extensive ploughing, and the re-allocation of land associated with the enclosure awards of the late eighteenth and early nineteenth century, obliterated many of the ancient field boundaries. Modern building development has also either destroyed or covered over the archaeological evidence of Roman occupation and associated land use. The evidence for Roman field patterns and sizes has, therefore, to be based entirely on those surviving fields which have had little usage since the Roman period, but even these may not be truly representative of the whole.[23]

A particular field system widely used throughout the Roman Empire was that of 'centuriation', in which areas of land were accurately surveyed and placed in a grid system for settlement and cultivation purposes. This systematic division of land was based on blocks of Roman *actus* squares in a grid which spanned at least 100 *actus* (or multiples of 100 *actus)* in one direction and, at right angles to this, divisions that would allow squares of 20 x 20 *actus* or rectangles of 20 x 21 *actus* and 20 x 24 *actus* to be achieved. The distinction between the square and rectantangular areas was that the squares were usually freehold tax-free colony areas, such as were often allotted to soldiers after a war, whereas the rectangles were state-owned land leased to tenants who were subject to tax.[24]

As it is conceivable that 'centuriation' was also used in Britain at some time during the Roman occupation between the first and fourth centuries, research has been undertaken by historians to establish the existence of the *actus* grid system. Those worthy of mention in Sussex were at West Blatchington,[25] Hurstpierpoint and the Ripe/Chalvington area.[26] Unfortunately, due to the scant nature of the evidence revealed, some of the claims have been the subject of debate and controversy. The system at West Blatchington was over a very limited area, and the field patterns at Hurstpierpoint were represented by slight impressions of precise regularity complemented with Roman pottery and other finds. The most convincing of all was that discerned in the vicinity of Ripe/Chalvington which covered a fairly large area where, according to Ivan Margary, the field outlines and hedgerows certainly indicated the presence of 'centuriation'.[27]

H. C. Brookfield in his article *The Estuary of the Adur* records that the pattern of field boundaries between Worthing and Littlehampton was rectangular in form and bore a striking similarity to the rectangular land division at Ripe studied by Margary.[28] In his book *The Sussex Landscape,* P. Brandon suggests that all such areas warranted further detailed investigation and it was this that led the authors to consider the field patterns in the Worthing area.

Detailed early maps of the Worthing area, such as Yeakell and Gardner's map of Sussex *c.* 1780 [reproduced as figure 4], confirm that the whole area was once subdivided in a rectangular pattern reflective of 'centuriation'. To ascertain if there was any evidence some correlation between the overlay grid and the surviving ancient boundaries and

Fig. 4 *Yeakell and Gardner's map of c. 1780*

to substantiate that these field patterns were a Roman imprint, a photographically reproduced, true to scale copy of the 1875 six-inch-to-one-mile Ordnance Survey map of the area
was systematically searched, using a rectangular overlay grid based on Roman *actus*
measurements. If a system of 'centuriation' existed in the Worthing area, there should be

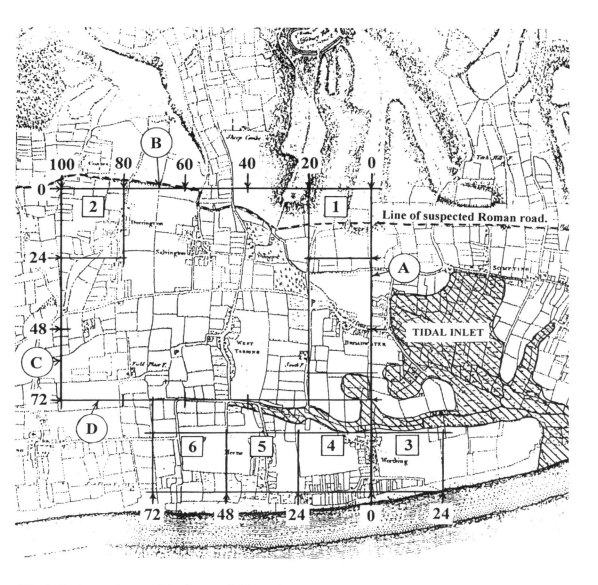

Fig. 5 *Conjectural map of the Roman field imprint*

topographical features on the map, having made due allowance for changes in field outlines, the effects of over 1,600 years of ploughing and the accuracy of the Roman surveyors compared with modern technology !

After many hours of research a correlation was discerned, and Figure 5 is a conjectural overlay of the Yeakell and Gardner map showing how the Roman geometric grid pattern was, in the authors' opinion, imprinted on the landscape of the Worthing area. Within an error of under 1%[29] the borders of the larger grid, marked A –D on Fig 5, were found to lie on, or very close to, ancient roads tracks or boundaries. Although two separate grids are shown on the map, they may well have been interconnected, and part of a much larger system extending to the west, perhaps as far as the Ferring Rife.

To the north-east of Broadwater Village is part of the prehistoric trackway which extended from Chanctonbury, past the east side of Cissbury, and down Charmandean Lane, marked 'A' on Fig.5. After crossing the modern A27 road it continued southwards along the ancient Quashetts footpath until it reached the tidal creek (called 'the Broadwater' by the Saxons). Modern geological evidence reveals that this ancient trackway probably marked the western extremity of the inlet and, as such, was an ideal base line for a Roman *actus* grid extending to the west. Running parallel to this base line, at a distance of 20 Roman *actus* to the west, lies the modern South Farm Road, which for centuries after the Roman occupation of Britain was a boundary between the manors of Broadwater and Offington. (see rectangle 1 on Fig. 5.)

At the western end of the grid, measuring 100 *actus* from Charmandean Lane, lies border 'C', which coincides with an ancient trackway running both north and south from a Roman road near Stanhope Lodge in Durrington. This track was probably of Celtic or Roman origin and is described by Ivan Margary as having 'some appearance of a metalled agger on its southward and derelict course past Stanhope Lodge.[30] It later became the parish boundary between Durrington and Goring. In 1924 Roman and Romano-British pottery was found near Durrington Manor house and about 30 yards [27.43 m] east of an old trackway running southwards past Field Place to the sea.[31] This old track is approximately 20 *actus* to the east of border 'C' (see rectangle 2 on Fig. 5). It is considered to be Celtic in origin and was used later by the Romans, and it has been suggested that a Romano-British dwelling had been close to the pottery that was found.

Although the distance between rectangles 1 and 2 on the grid measures 60 *actus,* suggesting further divisions of 20 *actus* (which would have been required for the geometric pattern of 'centuriation'), most of the ancient field patterns and boundaries in this part of the grid have unfortunately been obliterated by later field systems and modern development. Nevertheless, since the surviving evidence at either end of the grid supports divisions of 20 *actus* in an east–west direction, the approximate positions of the intermediate divisions are shown along the top of the perceived grid.

The southern extremity of the overall grid must have been influenced by the branch of the Teville stream that extended westwards from the tidal inlet. The ancient road separating the villages of Heene and West Tarring is situated just to the north of the stream, and strongly suggests a border of the grid (marked 'D' on Fig. 5). A measurement of 72 *actus* northwards (3 x 24 *actus*) results in a northern boundary to the grid just below the line of part of the old Roman road from Brighton to Chichester (marked C on Fig.5). Within this grid, sub-divisions of 20 x 20, 20 x 21 or 20 x 24 *actus* rectangles are all possible, but for illustration purposes rectangles of 20 *actus* (east to west) by 24 *actus* (north to south) are shown on Figure 5.

Although the series of rectangles was interrupted by water in a similar way to those discerned at Ripe in East Sussex, there is evidence to suggest that a further grid of *actus* rectangles also existed to the south of the Teville stream. The perceived grid is shown on Figure 5 and represents 4 rectangles of 20 x 24 *actus* (numbered 3-6) but with the 24 *actus* divisions aligned east to west. It would appear that the base for the southern grid ran between rectangles 3 and 4, and was the extension of the ancient Quashetts footpath and the present High Street (formerly part of Worthing Street).

The required correlation between the southern overlay grid and surviving ancient boundaries and topographical features is again evident. The western boundary of rectangle 4 (24 *actus* to the west of the base line) coincides with the later parish boundary between Worthing and Heene, and the western boundary of a further two rectangles of the same dimensions (marked 5 & 6 on Fig. 5) corresponds exactly to the later parish boundary between West Tarring and Goring. It is tempting to suggest that further rectangles possibly extended to the edge of the Ferring Rife, and even southwards on land now covered by the sea.

Evidence of Roman occupation in the area covered by rectangles 3 – 6 is confirmed by the number of archaeological finds recorded. Located on the lower Brighton Road, between the junction of Merton Road and Navarino Road, was the site of a Romano-British village thought to date from the first and second centuries AD.[32] According to Mr. Edward Sayers, based on the discovery of hot-air tiles found in the front garden of Fairlawn, the early Victorian villa that was demolished when the Museum was constructed in 1908, a Roman villa may have been located in the vicinity.[33] In September 1958 further evidence was found during the construction of an extension to the Museum.[34] In 1963, when rescue excavations were undertaken on the north side of Richmond Road on the site of the demolished St. Paul's Church schoolroom, several sherds of Romano-British pottery were also found.[35] An inscribed Roman stone was unearthed in Grand Avenue in 1901 together with Roman flue-tiles and roof stone etc.[36] In 1826 and 1828 Roman urns and coins were unearthed not far from Park Crescent.[37] Further to the west, a hoard of about 2100 coins was found in June 1958.[38] Numerous other Roman coins have been found in the Worthing area and these are recorded at Worthing Museum.

In the conclusion of a recent archaeological report, prepared in connection with the re-development of a site on the south-western corner of North Street and High Street, it is stated that

'In the Roman period, this area is likely to have formed part of a field system, with the few Roman sherds found on the site resulting from manuring'.[39]

Whether this field system was part of 'centuriation' has to remain conjecture. Unfortunately all that remains of the perceived Roman Imprint is limited parts of the fossilized outlines of the grid, and during the past hundred years even these have almost been obliterated by redevelopment. However, it cannot just be a coincidence that the measured distances between the various ancient boundaries equate to known Roman measurements. For there is no logical reason why the system of 'centuriation' that had been used elsewhere in Europe was not also used on the fertile coastal plain of Sussex.

During the second half of the fourth century AD, the rural economy in Roman Britain started to collapse. From 383 AD, the army in Britain was gradually reduced as units left to support pretenders to the post of Emperor.[40] Without an army to maintain security, peace and Imperial authority, the civilian population became self governing. The wealthy villa-owners were unable to prevent their slaves from deserting. Without a controlled labour force crops could not be harvested and estate management was destroyed.[41] Money no longer reached the country and fell out of circulation as it was lost or hoarded. As the monetary system failed, the goods which required coinage as the medium of exchange when traded were no longer produced and as the mechanisms of production, exchange and taxation ceased to operate the period of Roman culture in Britain finally came to an end.[42]

The date of 410 AD, confidently used by both archaeologists and historians as the end of Roman rule in Britain, is now being questioned. Modern research has shown that the surviving written records do not provide either a coherent or credible record of what happened during the fifth century and are not, therefore, a reliable source upon which to construct a considered account of what really happened. Historical sources naturally had a strong influence on the interpretation of archaeological evidence, and few attempts have been made to examine the period on the basis of archaeological material alone, without the prejudice inherent in the documentary sources.[43]

A very recent archaeological find in the Worthing area may provide more credible evidence as to the date of the end of Roman rule. In April 1997 a Roman coin hoard of 23 gold *solidi*, 25 silver coins and a quantity of silver bullion was unearthed at Patching to the north west of Worthing. Its suggested burial date of the late 460's places it as the latest hoard of Roman coins found to date in Britain, and this is possibly a more realistic date for the final departure of the Romans from the Worthing area.[44]

2. MEDIEVAL WORTHING

The interval between the end of Roman authority in Britain and the Domesday Survey of 1086 remains the subject of continuing academic debate. Recent critical archaeological opinion has cast doubts over the traditional interpretation of a fifth-century invasion and terms such as 'refugees' and 'boat people' have begun to replace the former ideas of 'Germanic mercenaries' and warriors arriving in Britain.[1]

The Sussex coastline of the fifth century was very different to the fairly smooth bay of today. Technically a 'coastline of submergence', it originally possessed great irregularity, being penetrated by tidal inlets in the vicinity of Pagham, Bognor, Ferring and Worthing, all of which are evidenced by the tracts of alluvium which clearly identify their former location.[2]

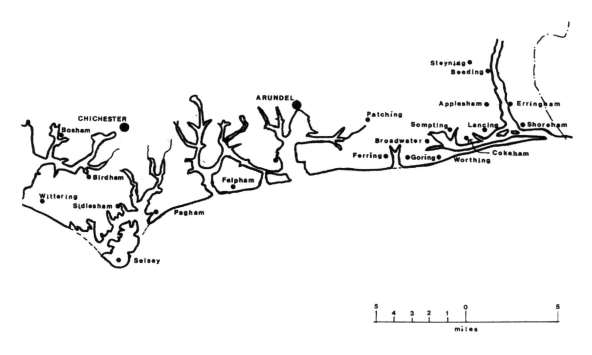

Fig. 6 *Conjectural map of fifth-century Sussex coastline*
(based on Yeakell and Gardner's map of c.1780 and work by Ballard)

The fifth-century coastline of Sussex was very similar to the flooded homelands the Anglo-Saxons had left on the North German and Frisian coast. It is, therefore, highly probable that these migrants, who crossed from Europe in draft boats, settled the wide river estuaries and tidal lagoons they encountered in Sussex. Indeed the potential fertility of the previously cleared and cultivated land, coastal accessibility and a plentiful supply of water, all available on the peninsula of land adjacent to the *'braden-waetere'*, must have been a major determinant in the selection of the sites of initial settlement.

Although it is rare to find evidence of early Saxon settlement, as the decayed timber houses and buildings lie beneath the many layers of subsequent rebuilding, an archaeological evaluation in 1997, prior to the construction of the modern two-storey office building for the Environment Agency in Little High Street, Worthing, revealed

'evidence of a moderate concentration of either Late Bronze Age or Saxon and later medieval activity in the form of pits, postholes and ditches.'[3]

On the basis of the artefacts found, the interim archaeological report suggests that there was

'a concentration of 10th century activity in the central area of the site with a continuity of boundaries being cut and re-cut across the central and south-eastern areas of the site.'

As these features were of no great depth the report concludes that these shallow ditches and gullies were probably used for either drainage or temporary boundary demarcation. Traces of similar boundary demarcation trenches were detected during excavations of the early Saxon settlement at Bishopstone in East Sussex[4] and at Charlton in Hampshire, where the boundaries enclosed a number of buildings.[5]

Like Bishopstone the Saxon settlement site at Worthing was surrounded on three sides by water and looked out over the English Channel. Because of the similarities it is the authors' opinion that the site in Little High Street may well have been the location of an initial fifth-century Saxon settlement.

The site at Worthing was ideally situated to gain access to the resources of the surrounding land and sea. It is evident from the later recorded name of 'Bovewoods Furlong'[6] in the Worthing common fields, and the field names to the north of the Teville stream and east of the 'Quashetts' - 'Southwoods', 'West Woods' and 'Chesswood' - that, the essential resource of woodland, needed to provide fuel, pasture for stock, timber for house building and for making ploughs and other tools[7] was close by on the peninsula of land that lay between the *'braden-waetere'* and the sea. Most of the low lying land near the Teville stream, which was later to become the Teville Common, would have been under water. This would have provided a natural harbour, and this may well have been the site of 'Worthing harbour' recorded in 1300.[8] The large fields of the Roman 'centuriation' geometric grid immediately surrounding the site had only recently been abandoned and were immediately available for exploitation by a society whose economy and related social structure was singularly focused on agricultural endeavour.

Although the Saxon immigrants probably settled on the land previously cultivated during the Roman occupation of Britain, and may well have continued to cultivate some of the fields of the Roman *actus* grid,[9] the economy of their settlements was very different. Whereas the Romans had been engaged in the production of food for a market, archaeological evidence has revealed the migrating Saxon farmers to be self sufficient, part of a subsistence society, where the unit of production and consumption was the family. Not only did agriculture provide virtually all the basic necessities of life, it was also the source of the raw materials used in the manufacture of 'consumable' products. It would appear that the family units were nuclear, comprising just parents, grand parents and children. Each family was, however, usually related to a wider circle of 'kindred' who probably lived on adjoining farms.[10] It is, therefore, not inconsistent to suggest that an initial fifth-century settlement at Worthing probably consisted of a number of households, whose buildings were separated one from another by either the ditches or fenced enclosures discerned by the archaeologists during their recent evaluation of the site in Little High Street.

Place-name evidence provides a further insight into the Saxon landscape and settlement pattern, as distinct variations in the spatial distribution and chronology of Saxon settlement are evident from recent studies that have re-evaluated this difficult and often controversial source.

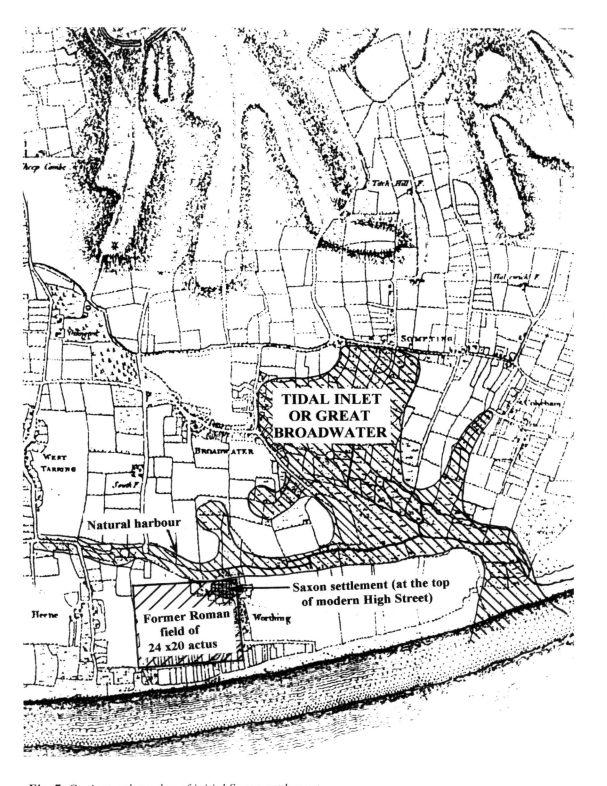

Fig. 7 *Conjectural overlay of initial Saxon settlement*

As can be seen in Fig.8, while place names ending in the suffix -*ham* predominate on the coastal plain to the west of the River Arun, very few occur between the Rivers Arun and Adur. In direct contrast, with the exception of West Wittering located on the Selsey peninsula, and Climping located to the west of the River Arun, all the other -*ingas* coastal settlements in West Sussex are grouped in a distinct enclave on the fertile brick-earth soils at the eastern end of the coastal plain and the rich alluvial deposits of the Adur basin.[11]

Toponymic interpretation relies on the assumption that each particular ancient place-name suffix is significant, and current research now suggests that it is those settlements ending with the suffix -*ham* that represent the initial colonisation of the fifth and sixth centuries.[12] While this interpretation questions the validity of the authors' premise that the settlement in Little High Street is of late fifth- or sixth-century origin, it must be inconsistent to argue that the Saxons, who crossed from eastern Europe in draft boats, did not also establish the -*ingas* settlements alongside the wide tidal lagoons they would have first encountered to the east of the River Arun.

It is, however, acknowledged that the pattern of Saxon settlement did not remain static, as had been previously thought. John Dodgson's interpretation therefore has possibly more credence. In his opinion the predominance of -*ingas* place names to the east of the Arun Basin records a post-eighth-century overlay that masks a former pattern of settlement similar to that to the west of the River Arun. This may well obscure the existence of earlier settlements that were probably known by different place names. Indeed, the surviving, albeit isolated, -*ham* settlements of Erringham, Shoreham and Cokeham may well evidence the residue of initial settlement to the east of the River Arun.[13]

Detailed research of the correlation between tenth-century land ownership and the -*ingas* and -*ham* settlements[14] reveals that this fundamental change in the pattern of settlement may have been determined by local influences, as the development of strong seigneurial control was initially limited to the more populated area at the eastern end of the coastal plain. Based on the tentative conclusions derived from archaeological fieldwork and documentary evidence, it would appear that there had, by the eighth century, been a distinct shift from the former family-orientated subsistence farming to intensive localised agricultural exploitation. During the middle and late Saxon period the former bonds of 'kinship', which had tied blood relations into the mutually supportive groups of initial colonisation, had gradually been eroded. As a result the fundamental social structure of the former self-sufficient family units of both production and consumption became weakened. Coincident with this radical change in the structure of Saxon society was an equally radical change in the pattern of Saxon settlement. Both land, and the attendant power to control it, was gradually being devolved from the King into the hands of the Church and the Saxon nobility.[15] The rather modest dues that had once been collected to sustain the King and his household were now diverted to the benefit of a 'landlord' who was not necessarily a noble, but either held the land directly from the Crown or was himself a tenant of the King.[16] Unlike the former collective tributary payments of food, which were borne by each settlement of related family groups, the dues or rents were now paid by individuals to the lord of their estate as either cash payments, through labour services or 'boon-work' such as ploughing or harvesting. Although the original sense of the word 'boon' was favour, through 'custom and practice' even these tasks eventually became compulsory.[17]

Exactly when the Saxon family farms consolidated into village communities under manorial control remains unclear, but by the ninth century Steyning, accessible by water, and lying at the head of the wide tidal estuary of the River Adur, had become the centre of the royal estates that encompassed both the densely populated Adur Valley and the -*ingas* settlements of the eastern coastal plain. Not only had the land been intensively exploited, the foundation of a permanent Saxon mint at Steyning in *c*. 1020 substantiates that this

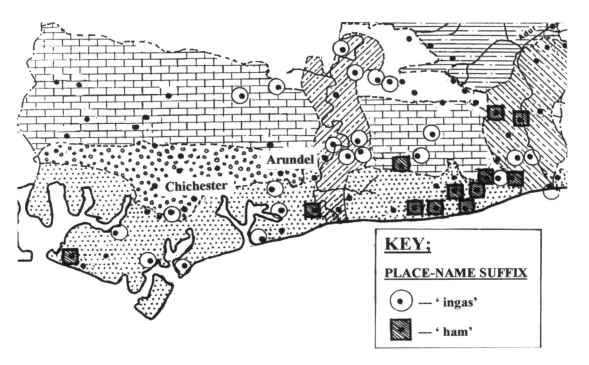

Fig. 8 *Distribution of place names on the Sussex coastal plain*
    (derived from the medieval form of the name in the 'Domesday' text)

particular area had already moved to a cash economy based on both agriculture and com-merce.[18] This post eighth-century overlay of manorial influence clearly laid down a frame-work of social structure that was firmly bound by manorial custom, and its institution as a remnant of the late Saxon period remained the basis of socio-economic relationships for many centuries. It is clearly evident that the enclave of -*ingas* place-names, at the eastern end of the coastal plain both represent and recall' this subsequent phase of colonisation. It would appear that Mawer and Stenton were correct when they suggested that the suffix -*ing*, from the Old English -*ingas*,

> 'shows at the very least that the settlements to which they applied came into being as
> communities and not single farms, and that they stand in sharp contrast to a terminal
> like -*ham* or *tun* preceded by a personal name in the possessive case.'[19]

Although most of the mints established during the Saxon period were located at the main commercial centres, it is now generally accepted that an emergency mint was established within the Iron Age fort at Cissbury for a brief period in the early eleventh century prior to the foundation of the more permanent mint at Steyning.[20]

In most instances the evidence for identifying the location of Saxon mints has been almost entirely derived from the coins themselves,[21] and in the late 1950's it was suggested that the words '*SITHE*', *SITHESTER*' and '*SITHMES*' (found on pennies of Ethelred II and Cnut, 1009 – 1023 AD) referred to a mint named '*SITHESTBURGH*' or '*SITHMESTBURGH*' The normal development of these words as a place name would lead to '*SIZBURY*' which is consistent with the old forms of the spelling found on seventeenth- and eighteenth-century maps, and is almost identical with the pronunciation of the name Cissbury today. It appears that '*SITH(M)EST*' means 'latest' or 'last', meaning late. Both forms of the name of the mint therefore mean 'the last stronghold'.[22] It is therefore linguistically plausible that the words on the coin refer to the Iron Age hill fort at Cissbury.

If the place name has been correctly identified, the Iron Age fort at Cissbury was not unique in being utilised as an emergency mint when the Saxons were forced to retreat from the intermittent attacks of the Danish Vikings during the last few years of Ethelred's reign. The mints at Walton and Ilchester were also transferred to the nearby Iron Age forts of 'Old Sarum' and 'Cadbury'.

Fig. 9 Saxon coin from Cissbury mint (scale twice full size)

Unlike the other emergency mints that had been transferred from commercial centres, Cissbury appears to have been newly created and was probably the precursor of the Saxon mint established at Steyning in *c.* 1020[23]. It has been suggested that, following the closure of the mint at Cissbury, the dies used for minting coins there were removed to Scandinavia and re-used there.[24] The new Saxon mint at Steyning continued to contribute on a small scale to most, if not all, of the coin issues up to the end of the reign of William II.[25]

The Domesday text still remains the vital documentary link between the later medieval period and the still relatively obscure centuries of the Saxon era. It records that by the end of the tenth century, and perhaps even earlier, there were two Saxon estates at Worthing: The entries are as follows:

In BRIGHTFORD Hundred

> Robert also holds **'Ordinges'** [Worthing] from William. 7 Freeholders held it from Earl Godwin. Then it answered for 11 hides; now Robert has 9 hides. They paid tax for 2 hides. Land for 3 ploughs. In lordship 2 ploughs; 6 villagers and 9 smallholders with 1 plough. 1 slave; meadow, 7 acres. Value before 1066, later and now 100s.
> Robert holds **'Mordinges'** [Worthing] from William. $1^1/_2$ hides Leofwin held it from the King. It paid tax for $^1/_2$ hide. 1 villager and 5 smallholders. Meadow $^1/_2$ acre. The value is and was 12s.[26]

Whereas most of the late Saxon estates had been sub-divided into the 'demesne' (farmed by the lord using labour services and 'boon' works due him by his tenants) and the land farmed by the tenants to sustain their families, the consolidation of the cultivated land at Worthing into the manor of 'Ordinges' appears to have been purely a fiscal arrangement. According to Marian Frost the seven freehold tenants at 'Ordinges' held this Saxon estate from Earl Godwin, the father of King Harold and father-in-law of King Edward the Confessor, who had married his daughter Edith[27]

> 'as an hereditary and perpetual estate, free to dispose of it by gift or sale, but subject to the common and constant land tax of hidage.'[28]

This again clearly implies that this particular settlement pre-dates the late eighth- and early ninth-century overlay of seigneurial control. That there were seven freeholders also appears to be very significant for, as can be seen from Fig. 10, the sub-division of a square measuring 16 Roman *actus* by 7 results in an acre equal to the 'notional' or 'customary acre' which persisted at Worthing until the early nineteenth century.

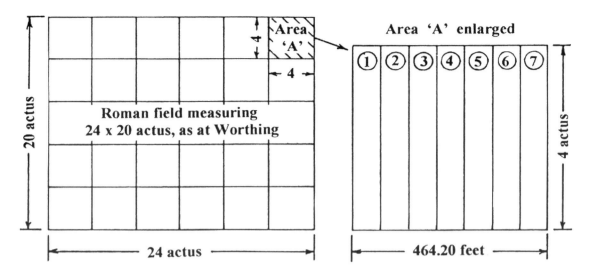

If the 7 Saxon freeholders at Worthing (recorded in the Domesday text) simply divided all the 4 actus squares into 7 equal strips, then each strip would measure 464.2 feet long x 66.31 feet wide. Using the English rod size of 16.5 feet , the strips are 28 rods long and 4 rods wide , a ratio of 7:1. The area of each strip is 464.2 feet times 66.31 feet divided by 43,560 (number of square feet in an acre) which equals 0.70 (ie about two thirds) of a statute acre. Chapter 3 relates this to the 'customary acre' at Worthing.

Fig. 10 *Conjectural division of the Roman field pattern into 'customary acres'*

The area of land that constituted a 'hide' when the Domesday text was compiled still remains controversial. Some historians consider it to be merely a fiscal assessment, not surveyed or even paced out, but simply used to evaluate land for tax purposes.[29] Others have suggested, based on evidence from the seventh and eighth centuries, that a 'hide' represents the amount of land a man needed to feed his family. Morris, in the Appendix to his translation of the Domesday entries for Sussex, suggests that it normally meant a number of acres, usually (but not always), 120 acres.[30] The simple, but pertinent, mathematical exercise of dividing the recorded acreage of 584 statute acres[31] for the township of Worthing in 1871 before it absorbed the surrounding villages within its boundaries, by the total number of 'hides' for both manors at Worthing [10.5], results in a 'hide' being approximately equal to only 56 statute acres or 80 customary acres.

Each manor's economic survival was dependent upon the amount of land available and it has been suggested that the term 'ploughland' represented an estimate of arable capacity.[32]   On the assumption that a 'ploughland' was equal to the area of a 'hide' the amount of land under cultivation on the larger manor of 'Ordinges' was :

In Lordship	2 ploughs = 2 hides = 112 statute acres	
Villagers and Smallholders	1 plough = 1 hide = 56 statute acres	

TOTAL	168 statute acres

This is very similar to the area of *c.* 150 acres for a Roman field of 20 x 24 *actus*.[33] While the smaller Saxon population undoubtedly reduced pressure on the land that had been so extensively cultivated in the Roman period, and scrub and woodland may have overgrown the fields which were no longer cultivated, continuity of land usage of one of the 20 x 24 *actus* squares is clearly evident. This may well be the single common field, recorded as the 'Worthingfield' in the manorial survey of the Manor of Broadwater dated 1300.[34]

While it has to remain conjectural, all the foregoing archaeological, documentary and toponymic evidence supports the authors' contention that the origins of the settlement called 'Ordinges' in the Domesday text pre-dates the late eighth- and early ninth-century overlay of seigneurial control. It is also plausible that part of the former Roman geometric *actus* grid field system of 'centuriation' was continuously exploited for over five hundred years by the descendants of the Saxon migrants that settled the late fifth-century site in Little High Street.

The smaller Saxon manorial estate of 'Mordinges' was held prior to 1086 by Earl Godwin's son, Leofwin, who was the brother of King Harold,[35] and this estate appears to have been part of the larger manor of 'Ordinges' until the late tenth century. As the northern end of modern Chapel Road and North Street formed part of an ancient roadway that skirted the extremity of the Saxon settlement that was to become the Domesday estate of 'Ordinges', it is not inconsistent to suggest that modern Warwick Street and South Street, which formed the final route to the sea as part of the same ancient roadway, also skirted the smaller Saxon estate of 'Mordinges'.

The settlement pattern and social structure of the Saxon landholdings recorded in Domesday had already passed beyond the colonial stage and were the culmination of at least six centuries of pioneering effort. When the Norman clerks prepared the Domesday Book the south eastern coastal area of England was already one of the longest inhabited and most populous areas of England. Layer upon layer of inherited man-made feature were already etched into its varied and diverse landscape.

Following the Norman Conquest, as a direct result of the radical re-allocation of land, the former pattern of Saxon independent tenurial ownership was overlaid by large 'territorial estates' within a contrived national and regional administrative structure, controlled by the King through his appointed 'tenants-in-chief'. As land undoubtedly remained the major resource for wealth, and as such reflected both status and power, the re-distribution of land by King William following the Norman Conquest concentrated both in the hands of a relatively small elitist class of Norman barons and ecclesiastics.

It was during this early Norman period that Sussex attained its greatest importance in relation to other counties and as Armstrong records,

> For over 150 years it was the main highway from England to the Continent – a bridge connecting the estates of the Norman nobility in England with Normandy.[36]

For strategic reasons, and to control his lines of communication with Europe, by 1086 William had placed Sussex under the control of two powerful overlords. The most powerful of these feudal barons was Roger of Montgomery, who was overlord of a singular rape that encompassed over 60% of West Sussex prior to its sub-division into the rapes of Chichester and Arundel in the mid-thirteenth century. Within this rape he held over eighty manors, leased singularly or in groups to lesser figures in the Norman hierarchy. The Rape of Bramber was controlled by William de Braose, who attended William in his invasion and conquest of England. On the division of the Saxon 'Spoil' he was rewarded with the remaining 41 Manors in Sussex, besides others in Hampshire and Dorset.[37]

The remnant of the earlier Saxon coastal defence system was re-shaped to ensure that no other invader could repeat William the Conqueror's own success. Possibly in return for

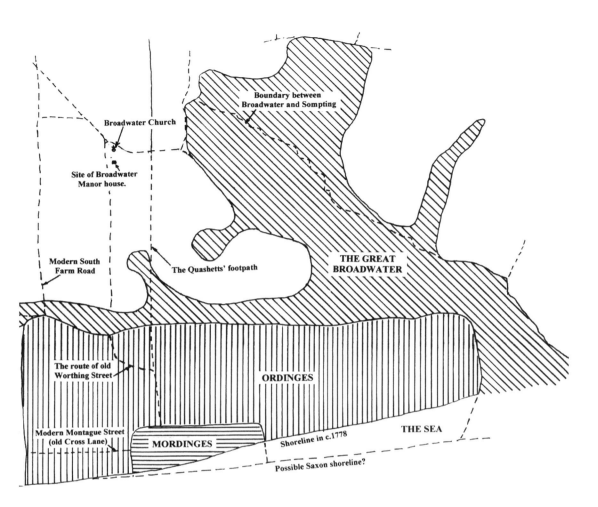

Fig. 11 *Conjectural overlay of post tenth-century Saxon estates of 'Ordinges' and 'Mordinges'*

protecting the foreshore within the boundaries of the Rape of Bramber, William de Braose was granted the 'right of wreck' to be taken *'infra honorem'* or *'infra baronian'*.[38] Lords who held this 'right of wreck' or 'wreck of the sea' were entitled to the best anchor and cable (the heavy rope or chain for mooring or anchoring a ship) of every foreign ship and the best cable of every British ship that was stranded or driven ashore. These had, however, to be kept for a year and a day, and if anyone could satisfactorily prove it was legally their property within that time the goods had to be returned, after all costs had been paid. From the precedent revealed in the surviving charters of the early Norman Kings the 'foreshore' clearly passed to those who held the coastal manors in Sussex, as 'under-tenants' of William de Braose,[39] but it is not clear when and how the 'right of wreck' also became vested in these coastal manors.

        In the Hundred Rolls (1274/5) for the County of Sussex, William de Braose is recorded as having 'wreck of the sea' for the Port of Shoreham, whereas his under-tenants, John de Camoys (Broadwater Manor), Nigel de Brooke (Lancing Manor), Godfrey de Faulkenor (Heene Manor) and Hugh de Buscy (Kingston Manor) as lords of their respective manors have 'wreck of the sea' against their lands.[40] However, towards the end of the thirteenth century the same lords were challenged over their 'right of wreck' and it was determined that the 'right of wreck' was vested in their 'over-lord' William de Braose.

Nigel de Brooke and Hugh de Buscy were fined for false claims and John de Camoys and his wife Margaret were discharged since they did not 'usurp upon the King or his ancestors'. It was however re-affirmed that William de Braose had 'wreck of the sea' over the sea coast in his barony, and accordingly he was discharged.[41]

Goods washed up on the beach could not be claimed as 'wreck of the sea' unless they were cast upon the shore between the high and low water mark and, if they formed part of a ship or its cargo out of which *none of the crew or any domestic animal escaped alive'*, they became the absolute property of the person in whom the 'right of wreck' was vested.[42]

Both the assumption to goods as 'right of wreck' and the assertion to the 'right of the foreshore' at Worthing were considered in 1332 when Ralph de Camoys (Lord of the Manor of Broadwater) sued Stephen de Peshale and others for seizing goods from a ship wrecked off the coast of Worthing. Stephen de Peshale's defence was that he held the hamlet of Worthing, which was part of Broadwater Manor in 'right of Alina his wife', as part of the barony of Bramber. As the hamlet of Worthing was situated on the coast he contested that he, in right of his wife, therefore held the 'right of wreck'. Stephen de Peshale had kept the goods on this assumption until one of the merchants, who had survived, claimed them. Although Stephen de Peshale returned the goods, the jury found him guilty and awarded damages of 64 marks as the goods were not legally 'right of wreck'. His claim to the right of the foreshore was, however, unchallenged.[43]

Many historians, when considering the impact of the Norman Conquest, have suggested that the arrival of William, although a significant event in English history, did not herald any major changes in the economic or social life of those who lived and worked on the various manors. Although foreign lords had taken over, in many respects life continued as before. This view is possibly a little too simplistic, for significant changes had occurred. As the Domesday text reveals, both the former manor at Broadwater and the two former Saxon estates at Worthing now formed part of the large Norman 'Fief' or multiple manor estate held by Robert le Savage, as an under-tenant of William de Braose. By amalgamating these former independent Saxon estates and manors into a single enterprise, Robert le Savage was able to both manage and fully exploit the potential of the land in each of the various manors under his control. Most of his arable holdings were on the fertile coastal plain between the Arun and the Adur. These provided not only the arable land on which to concentrate his main cereal crops, but also vast downland sheepwalks, while his Wealden forest edge holdings provided further pasture land and the woodland resources so essential for economic stability.[44]

Robert le Savage's multiple estate was controlled by his descendants until at least 1268, [45] and in 1269 all the land at both Broadwater and Worthing passed to Sir John de Camoys and his wife Margaret.[46] In 1285 Margaret de Camoys left her husband to live with Sir William Paynel. It would appear, however, that having done so, in fear of the indoctrination of mediaeval Christianity, she considered her actions had placed her soul at risk. The medieval church considered 'salvation of the soul' was a commodity that could be bought by the simple expedient of bestowing gifts on the Church, often in the form of grants of land. All over England abbots, priors, prioresses and abbesses were acquiring estates made up entirely of gifts 'for the good of my soul and the soul of my ancestors'[47] and the grant of land in both Broadwater and Worthing to Easebourne Priory in 1291 would appear to have been made for the salvation of Margaret de Camoys' soul! In 1295, however, three years before Sir John de Camoys' death, the then Prioress of Easebourne repaid the generous gift of the priory's benefactress, for she was one of those who, on oath, cleared Margaret de Camoys of a charge of adultery.[48]

The Priory of Easebourne held these lands until the dissolution of 1536[49] when they were granted by Henry VIII to the treasurer of his household, Sir William Fitzwilliam, at which point they became the 'Manor of Worthing'. The Court books for the manor of Worthing reveal, however, that the land granted to the Priory of Easebourne at the end of the thirteenth century was not a composite block, but individual enclosures or 'closes' and strips of land in the common or open fields. In reality, the grant made to the Priory was the allocation of the revenue from certain of the manorial tenants, whose land was already dispersed throughout the arable land and pasture of the composite manor held by descendants of the le Savage family since Domesday.

Two other religious houses were also granted land at Worthing during the thirteenth century. William de Bernehouse gave land in Worthing to the hospital he had founded at Cokeham in Sompting in c. 1278,[50] and this passed with the hospital to Hardham Priory in 1351.[51] By the seventeenth and eighteenth centuries it appears that this land had become part of Cokeham Manor and is recorded as amounting to c. 56 acres in the Worthing Inclosure documentation.[52] Tortington Priory also held lands in Worthing and Shoreham by 1291 and this produced an annual rent of 4 shillings.[53]

These bequests of land to the Church, and their subsequent re-distribution at the Reformation, explain why the various old enclosures, together with the strips in the open fields at Worthing, were under the control of more than one manor. Indeed, as will be shown later in this book, the closes or sites that lay either side of the ancient route of old Worthing Street were variously held from Broadwater, Worthing, Lancing or Cokeham manors, or were glebe-land under the control of the Church.

3. THE AGRICULTURAL AND FISHING HAMLET

The definition of a hamlet - a small community, usually without a church, that shared a parish with an adjoining village[1] - accurately describes the settlement at Worthing from the late Saxon period until the late eighteenth century. Until 1803 Worthing was an integral part of the ancient Parish of Broadwater and the *Victoria History of the County of Sussex* describes the pre-nineteenth-century settlement as

> 'a small agricultural and fishing hamlet of lesser importance than the neighbouring village of Broadwater.'[2]

Although Worthing did not have its own church until the early nineteenth century, a chapel is recorded in 1291. This was demolished by 1635 but even though there has been much speculation over its location the site has still to be positively identified.[3]

In 1566 there were thirty households recorded in the hamlet. Approximately forty people are listed in the 1664/5 Hearth Tax returns[4] and probably about thirty of the overall

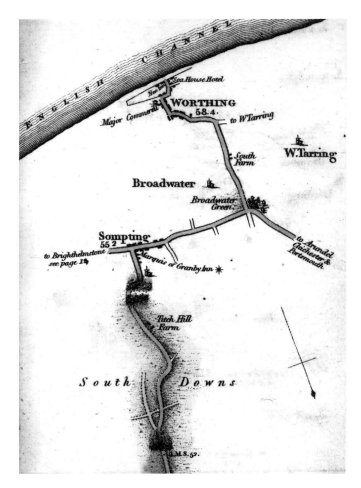

Fig. 12 *Pre-nineteenth-century coaching route to Worthing*

total of sixty families recorded at Broadwater in 1724, actually lived at Worthing.[5] Unfortunately, to date, no detailed pre-eighteenth-century map showing the location of the houses has been discovered. Even the accuracy and siting of the buildings shown on Yeakell and Gardner's map of *c.* 1780 should be viewed with caution, as these very small-scale county maps appear to have been produced primarily to depict the county's overall topography. As a consequence the location of most of the houses in the pre-nineteenth-century hamlet of Worthing can only be conjecture. Documentary evidence does, however, reveal that the largest group was of post-medieval houses almost certainly located on, or very near, the site of the Saxon settlement at the northern end of modern High Street. Another smaller group was possibly located nearer the sea, to the south of modern Warwick Street and Brighton Road, and houses may also have existed on either side of Cross Lane (modern Montague Street).

Before the introduction of turnpike roads at the beginning of the nineteenth century, those travelling to Worthing from the north of the county had to travel on a track over the South Downs, that was in part the ancient route between Arundel and Steyning. Like many of the roads in Sussex it was just a series of winding country lanes and was in several places totally unconnected.[6] Having arrived at Broadwater the only approach for vehicular traffic to Worthing was down Brooksteed Lane, which ran on the western side of Broadwater Green before following the line of modern South Farm Road southwards. After crossing the Teville Stream anyone visiting or returning to Worthing would then have continued down 'Worthing Street', first easterly along what is today Teville Road, then south into the northern end of modern Chapel Road. They would then have turned east again into modern North Street until they reached the heart of the pre-nineteenth-century hamlet either side of modern High Street. At the southern end of modern High Street Worthing Street ran both west and east. The western branch is today Warwick Street and South Street where it finally reached the sea. The eastern branch ran at an angle below the line of the present Brighton Road, until it turned sharply south towards the sea at a point just opposite the southern end of modern Selden Road.

Like most of the village streets that take the name of the village they served, Worthing Street was for centuries the main artery of the community at Worthing. As can be seen on Fig. 13, in distinct contrast to the labyrinth of roads that exist today, the only other road was Cross Lane (modern Montague Street) which extended from modern South Street to the boundary between Worthing and Heene.

From the early part of the nineteenth century, as the hamlet gradually became amalgamated into the town, the name Worthing Street gradually dropped out of use. New roads appeared and various sections of the street were re-named. To assist in the identification of these re-named sections letters are shown superimposed on Figure 13 at various points along its ancient route.

Section A to B [modern Teville Road] represents the north-western section of Worthing Street, which was also part of the ancient road to Tarring. In the early part of the nineteenth century the road between the southern side of Broadwater Bridge to Heene Road was known locally as 'Vapours Lane,'[7] the name probably originating from the mists that would have frequently collected along this stretch of low-lying and possibly marshy land. Between 1818 and 1836 the Worthing rate books refer to this section of the road as 'The Teville' and one of the earliest references to Teville Road is on the Hide Survey (1838). Because the majority of the land to the south of this section of the road was the open or common 'West Field' it could not be developed until after 1806, when it was re-allocated into private ownership under the 'Broadwater Inclosure Act'. In fact, no development took place until the mid-Victorian period. To the north of Worthing Street was the Teville (Teevil or Tevil) Common which, together with the Town Meads to the east, appears to have been reclaimed from a branch of the original, much wider, Teville stream which divided Broadwater from Worthing.

The 1875 Ordnance Survey map clearly shows that the source of the western branch of the Teville Stream originated in springs and ponds situated in and around the old Lincet Barn at West Tarring, the majority of which is currently the site of the West Tarring allotments. These springs linked together and ran southwards to meet the Tarring Road (then Tarring Lane). The resulting stream then continued in an easterly direction, first north and then south of Tarring Lane, eventually dividing to skirt the north and south edges of the Teville Common before discharging into the pond at its eastern end. From the pond the stream continued eastwards to meet the main stream (originally the great 'Broadwater') where it joined and flowed south-eastwards to empty into the sea between East Worthing and Lancing.

The old medieval port or harbour of Worthing is recorded in 1300 and 1493 and was a constituent member of the 'Port of Shoreham' in 1324.[8] Having thoroughly searched the existing maps and other available evidence, logic determines the most suitable and likely location for this old port was in and around the area that was later to become the Teville Common. The early Sussex coastline, which almost certainly extended much further southwards than today, contained many inlets and creeks. Several of these were navigable for some distance inland and were possibly used as harbours or shelters. Centuries of erosion and accretion have produced the fairly smooth bay we see today, as the continual and relentless eastward littoral drift sealed off or diverted these creeks, inlets and river mouths to the east. As early as the sixteenth century the old port of 'Pende' at Lancing was no longer usable and it appears that Worthing's port shared the same fate. During Tudor times a substantial amount of the marshy land from these sealed-off creeks and inlets was reclaimed for agricultural purposes and the Teville Common appears to be a possible example of this.

Ten farmers claimed common rights on the Teville Common in 1696[9] and John Evans, in the first known guide book for Worthing, quaintly describes the common as being,

'watered by the Teville and spotted with cattle belonging to the peasantry.'[10]

The number of animals allowed to pasture on the common was regulated by Broadwater's Manorial Court.

By 1814 Section B to C [northern end of modern Chapel Road] had been re-named North Street and, although it was soon to be connected with the 'New London Road' (Chapel Road), it was not until 1881 that a rate book records its change to 'Chapel Road (North end) late North Street'.

Section C to D [modern North Street] was recorded as 'Middle Street' between circa 1805[11] and 1810. Phillips' map shows it as 'West Street' and it probably remained as such until the name was transferred to the modern West Street which runs between Montague Street and the sea front.[12] This must have taken place prior to 1838 since Hide's survey of that date records this section under its present name of North Street.

Section D to E has been known as High Street from at least 1804[13] until the present day although, according to the plan of Worthing surveyed for the 1806 'Inclosure' it was marked as North Street, which would appear to be an error by the Surveyor, George Bassett. To the north of the point (marked D on Figure. 13) Worthing Street continued for a short distance before turning eastwards to serve a few more properties. Opposite the junction of this short section of street was another short section running westwards. This was known as 'Tanners Lane'[14] or 'Hamper's Lane' (modern Little High Street). Although the origin of 'Hamper's Lane' is uncertain, there was a William Hamper at Worthing who was elected Headborough in 1700 and he may have had some connection with this lane. Its earlier name of 'Tanners Lane' together with the two adjacent crofts immediately on the north, named 'Tanhouse Croft' and 'Tanners Croft', undoubtedly suggest a tannery may have existed nearby, possibly prior to the start of the Worthing Manorial Court Books in 1544.

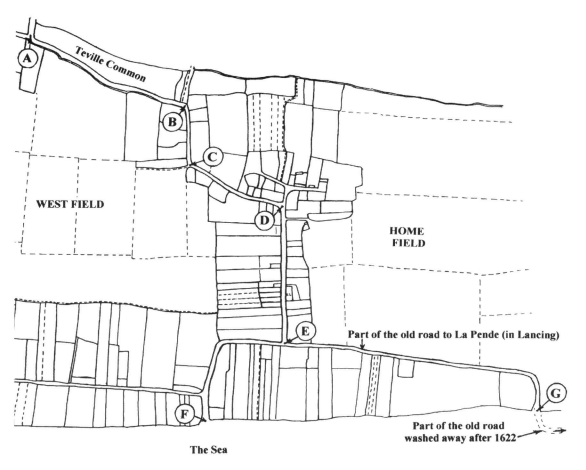

Fig. 13 *The route of old 'Worthing Street'*

Although the existence of a tanner has not been unearthed in the extensive research of the various records that still exist for Worthing, a tannery would have been vital from the medieval period for transforming cattle hides into leather for the manufacture of clothing, footware and equipment. As the tanning process produced strong and very unpleasant odours, it was usually sited on the outskirts of a settlement so that the normal prevailing winds would blow the smell away from the community. At Worthing the site was ideal since the smell would have, for the majority of the time, been diverted across the Broadwater and Sompting brooks. The nearby Teville stream was probably the source of the necessary water supply. Oak bark, which provided the tannin to convert the hide to leather, and cattle, preferably from a slaughter house, would also have been required.[15] It is interesting to note that there were several slaughter houses on 'Tanhouse Croft' from at least *c.* 1838 to 1898, perhaps indicating that there may also have been an earlier one on the site during the period the tannery was in use.

From the southern end of modern High Street is Section E to F, which terminates where the modern Pier Pavilion and Pier is located today. This section is today Warwick Street and South Street, both of which are recorded on the 1806 'Inclosure' map. In 1650 this section was referred to as 'Worthing Street'[16] but by the end of the eighteenth century (*c.* 1786) it was known as 'West Lane'. This section was an access road to the Worthing or Saltgrass Common, where the inhabitants pastured their animals, and the 'shingle beach' where the fishermen's huts and other buildings were located.

Modern Montague Street, which led towards Heene, was recorded as 'Cross Lane' in the eighteenth century. On either side of this lane were enclosed crofts of land which appear to have originated in the medieval period. The furlong located in the common 'West Field' immediately to the north of these crofts, named 'South Furlong' by the late eighteenth century, was known as 'Bove Crofts Furlong' during the seventeenth century. Since 'Cross Lane' provided the only access to these crofts, some of which contained houses and other buildings, it may have originally been known as 'Crofts Lane'. (A parallel example of this type of corruption is the modern 'Mash Barn Lane' in Lancing which was originally known as 'Marsh Barn Lane'.)

Heading in an easterly direction, from the southern end of modern High Street, is Section E to G, which also terminated at the sea. By the end of the eighteenth century this was all that remained of a road recorded some 200 years earlier in 1581 as 'a highway from Worthing to La Pende'[17] (South Lancing). It would, therefore, appear that from the medieval period there was a road linking the port of Worthing with the port of Pende in South Lancing. This road, which is still recorded on a map of 1622,[18] was later washed away.[19] By 1747 the surviving length of road was known as 'East Lane'. Between 1806 and 1808 a new road was laid out by the Worthing Town Commissioners, utilising part of this old road. This new road is the modern Brighton Road while any remains of the old road have long since been obliterated.

By the seventeenth century the greater part of the hamlet was still very rural in character. It was typical of ribbon development, with the majority of the farmsteads and cottages clustered either side of Worthing Street as it wandered its circuitous route to the sea. Apart from the narrow enclosed fields that adjoined both Worthing Street and Cross Lane, the remainder of the hamlet was divided into four large open or common fields.

Surveys of the manor of Broadwater dated 1300 and 1493[20] indicate that all the arable land at Worthing was then in a single common field called the 'Worthingfield'. In the authors' opinion this was the remnant of the Roman *actus* field pattern that had been subsequently farmed by the Saxons. Within this common or open field, so called because of the lack of hedges or fences in or around it, the arable land was subdivided into one-, half- and quarter-acre nominal strips which were grouped together into furlongs. Although the strips in each furlong were aligned in the same direction, strips in adjoining furlongs were often aligned in a different direction, to take into account the natural drainage of the land. The manorial tenants were allotted individual strips over a number of furlongs, the theory being that each received a share of the good and bad land. As the boundary between the strips was often only a raised 'balk' of land this ensured the system of agriculture used was based on co-operation since of necessity each strip within a particular furlong had to grow the same crop at the same time. There was no room for individualism in medieval agriculture!

The words furlong and acre are both of Saxon origin; furlong was derived from *furh* meaning a furrow (i.e. furrow-long) and acre or *aecer* meaning a field or sown land, from the Old Saxon *akker*, which itself was derived from the Latin *'agar'* meaning a field (with no notion of a definite area).[21] Since time immemorial the length of an acre was a furlong 40 rods long, this being the distance a team of eight oxen could pull a plough without requiring a rest or being out of breath. An acre was the amount of land which could be ploughed in a day, although in reality it was ploughed in a morning as it was 'custom and practice' to put the oxen out to pasture during the afternoon. This is consistent with the German *Morgen* (morning) which was the amount of land ploughed between day-break and the early afternoon.[22] Several attempts were made by government to standardise or control the size of an acre, seemingly without success, since in Sussex and elsewhere the recorded length of the rod (pole or perch) used to measure an acre varied between 14 and 20 feet.

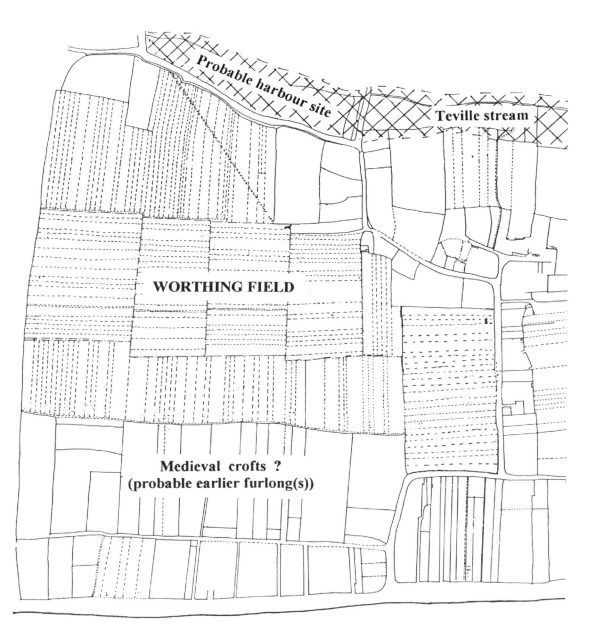

Fig. 14 *Orientation of Strips in 'Worthing Field'*

Although a 16-foot rod was used at both Ferring and West Tarring, to date no record has been found defining the length of rod used at either Worthing or Broadwater.

It has been summised that the size of an acre may have been influenced by the fertility and condition of the soil or indeed by earlier Roman and medieval measurements[23] as suggested earlier in this book. Research has also substantiated that the variations in size of the acre and rod were purely the result of 'local custom and practice' which was so entrenched that it resisted any changes either from the passage of time or Acts of Parliament. These local acres were known as 'customary acres' and research carried out on a number of early estate maps indicate that the area of a 'customary acre' on the West Sussex coastal plain was generally equal to about two-thirds of a statute acre.[24]

The area of a 'customary acre' can often be determined within a parish or manor if the ancient fields, whose names record their size, are compared with their later recorded statute measurement. The *Glebe Terrier* for Broadwater Parish, dated 1615, records two separate fields as the 'Upper' and 'Lower Nine Acres'. In both cases the later statute measurement was 6 acres. The '40 Acre Mead' in Worthing is recorded as such in both the *Broadwater Court Books* and the *c.* 1720 map of Broadwater. Subsequent statute measurement shows it to be 27.25 acres. Both these examples suggest the 'customary acre' in the Parish of Broadwater was equal to two-thirds of a statute acre.

At Worthing the open field system of agriculture continued until the 'Inclosure Act' of 1806 when a map was produced (presumably for use by the Enclosure Commissioners) detailing the names of the occupants and the 'customary acreage' of all the strips of arable land within the open fields. This provided the authors with a useful opportunity to carry out the simple mathematical exercise of totalling the acreage of all the strips from this map, and comparing it with the equivalent area in statute measurement shown on the Worthing Inclosure Map of 1805. Despite the passage of some 450 years since the late medieval period, and changes in agriculture and equipment etc., the results unequivocally show that, in parity with the research in other areas of the West Sussex coastal plain, a 'customary acre' at Worthing was 0.68 or two-thirds of a statute acre.[25]

A manorial tenant's holding was normally a 'virgate' or 'yardland' (sometimes called a 'wist' in East Sussex). Although a 'virgate' is often quoted as representing 30 acres it also must have varied according to the fertility of the soil, as did the acre. In *The South East from AD 1000*[26] it is suggested that in coastal Sussex the 'virgate' was considerably less than 30 acres: examples as low as 10 'customary acres' for the 'wist' are recorded in some East Sussex manors, the average size being about 12-14 statute acres. The 'virgate' of West Sussex was apparently no larger. It has been suggested that the reasons for this were

> 'a relatively dense population, the relative fertility of the soil and the importance of sheep grazing, and also the feasibility of more intensive cropping than that of the three-course rotation.'[27]

It would appear that by the introduction of legumes into the crop rotations, superior nutrient supplies were added to the soil, and fallow was virtually eliminated by the thirteenth century. Indeed in medieval England coastal Sussex along with North Kent was among the leading producers of legumes.[28]

The period between the two manorial surveys of Broadwater in 1300 and 1493 encompassed not only the 'Black Death', which ravaged the country in 1348, but also the subsequent plagues of 1361-2, 1387 and 1396 that followed it. Deterioration of the weather may also have contributed to several bad harvests and sheep and cattle diseases, all of which had a further adverse effect on the economy. As a result of the plagues there was a dramatic fall in population (figures quoted for the effects of the 'Black Death' generally range from a one-third to two-thirds decrease in population throughout the country). Labour became short, prices fell and costs rose. The Lord's 'demesne' shrank in size and many of the labour services required by the customary tenants were commuted to money payments, allowing the tenants more time to pursue their own work and gradually to obtain a higher standard of living as real wages improved. The more fortunate of the surviving tenants were able to take over the vacant holdings of those deceased and they, or their descendants, were able to take advantage of lower fixed rents for leased land by the end of the fourteenth century.[29]

Although there are no reliable records to show the direct effects of the plague in the Parish of Broadwater, there is no reason to believe that the local inhabitants escaped the catastrophe. Comparisons between the subsidies levied in 1378[30] and 1524[31] possibly indicate the long term effect, as there would appear to be no perceptible increase in

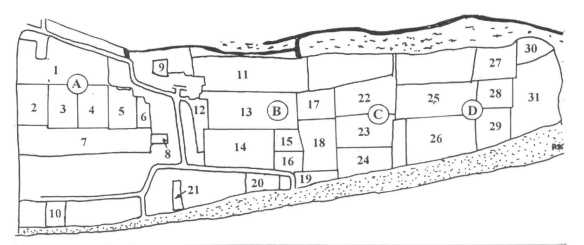

The diagram above shows A and B which represent the two original 24x20 Roman actus fields while C and D represent the eastern part of the 'Open Field' system at Worthing. Evidence suggests that when fields A and B were initially being worked , C and D were almost certainly wooded or waste lands. They were cleared for cultivation as population increased and more food was required. In the tables below the various names of the furlongs within the open fields are given together with supporting dates extracted from research material.

A= WORTHING FIELD 1300,1493;
=WEST FIELD C1560 TO 1806.

No.	Furlong
1	The Rent ,1651 to 1806.
2	Mark ,1653 to 1806.
3	Furlong next to Marke ,1658 ; Chapel Hill ,1805/6.
4	Middle Hill ,1665 to 1806.
5	East Hill ,1805/6.
6	Long Hill ,1805/6.
7	(A)Bove Crofts ,1653 to 1789 ; South 1805/6.
8	Gurr's Corner ,1665 to 1806.
9	North Town ,1688 to 1806.
10	Sea Field ? ,1653 ; West Sewells ,1805/6.

B=EAST FIELD C1560 ;
= EAST FIELD NEXT THE TOWNE ,1635 ;
= HOME FIELD , 1687 TO 1806.

No.	Furlong
11	Mead ,1616 to 1806.
12	The Butts , 1653 to 1806.
13	Middle , 1663 to 1806.
14	Myle/Mile ,1688 to 1806.
15	Broadlands , 1688 to 1806.
16	Shortlands , 1789 to 1806.
17	Yolme , 1653 to ?.
18	Thunderlands , 1688 to 1806.
19	Hemplands ? ,1635 ; Harebeaten Bank ,1805/6.
20	(Great) South Town ,1653 to 1806.
21	Little South Town ,1789 to 1806.

C=MIDDLE FIELD 1653 TO 1806

No.	Furlong
22	North , 1805/6.
23	Middle ,1789 to 1806.
24	Gore ,1688 ; South ,1805/6.

D=EAST-MOST FIELD ,C1560
=EAST FIELD ,1688 TO 1806.

No.	Furlong
25	(A)Bovewoods , Buffwoods ,1688 to 1806.
26	Gore ,1688 to 1806.
27	Brook , 1687 1806.
28	Millborough ,1789 to 1806.
29	Earth Pitt ,1687 to 1806.
30	Sandhill ,1789 ; Sandalls , 1805/6.
31	Myle ?, 1635 ; East or Long ,1805/6.

Fig. 15 *Development of the open fields*

population by 1524. This, combined with the two manorial surveys which show the continued use of <u>only</u> <u>one</u> open field for the intervening 193 years, perhaps says it all, since it is not until 1560 that an additional field is recorded as the 'East Common Field' on the eastern side of Worthing Street, opposite the former single common field now known as the 'West Common Field'.[32]

To the east of the hamlet lay the woodland and/or waste land, which had been an important source to the community of both fuel and building materials. At some time between 1560 and the seventeenth century, part of this woodland or waste was converted into arable land to form two more open fields, namely the 'Middle Field' and the 'Easternmost Field' [see Fig. 15]. A clue to the 'Easternmost Field's' former use is revealed on a c. 1805/6 map of Worthing, which records one of the furlongs in it as 'Buffwoods' or 'Bovewoods' (i.e. originally a furlong cleared above the woods). The 'East Field' was thereafter often referred to as the 'East field next to the town' to distinguish it from the more recent 'Easternmost Field'.

This situation prevailed at Worthing until the 'Inclosure Act' was implemented between 1806 and 1810. By then, the former 'Easternmost Field' had become the 'East Field' and the former 'East Field next to the town' had been renamed 'Homefield' (today commemorated by Homefield Park). A diagrammatic summary of the development of the various open fields at Worthing is reproduced as Figure 15, on which the various names of the open fields and furlongs are recorded, together with their former names.

Although detailed information concerning the inhabitants of the hamlet of Worthing is contained in documents dated between c. 1520 and 1800, the majority of the documents researched date from the beginning of the seventeenth century, when an overwhelmingly rural-based society was still to be found on the coastal plain of Sussex. The mid-seventeenth-century population for the whole of this region was probably no more than 14,000,[33] of which Worthing's contribution was probably no more than 200. There were only three reasonably sized towns, namely Chichester, Arundel and Shoreham, none of which could be described as highly industrial.

In recent years, following extensive detailed research and debate, historians have discerned that the different types of farming practices closely follow the topography of the various physiographic regions. In general terms there are basically three broad farming categories: arable, mixed, or pastoral, and it is from these that the many regional and local variations or sub-types are derived.[34] Broadwater Parish, with 'open field' settlements at both Broadwater and Worthing, is one of 59 coastal plain parishes between Southwick on the east and West Thorney on the west, which the authors consider fell within a farming region where mixed farming predominated.[35]

Possibly the most useful documents for those seeking information on people and their property are the surviving probate inventories and wills, which provide a valuable insight into the lifestyle of those who lived on the coastal plain during the seventeenth and eighteenth centuries. An inventory of the deceased's goods and chattels was required in order to grant the probate of a will, or at the issuing of letters of administration if the person died intestate. The inventory was supposed to be compiled by a competent person who was deemed qualified to assess the value of the deceased's 'movable' estate, which in most instances excluded freehold land, long term leases and buildings.[36] In reality the assessors were invariably not qualified, and were the neighbours and/or friends of the deceased. Although the surviving probate inventories represent probably no more than a quarter of the population, an idea of the lifestyle and social standing of those who lived and worked on the coastal plain of Sussex during the period 1600 to 1699 can be derived from a detailed study and analysis of the 'goods and chattels' listed in the 3034 probate inventories, deposited at the West Sussex Record Office, for the 59 relevant coastal plain parishes. As only 108 of

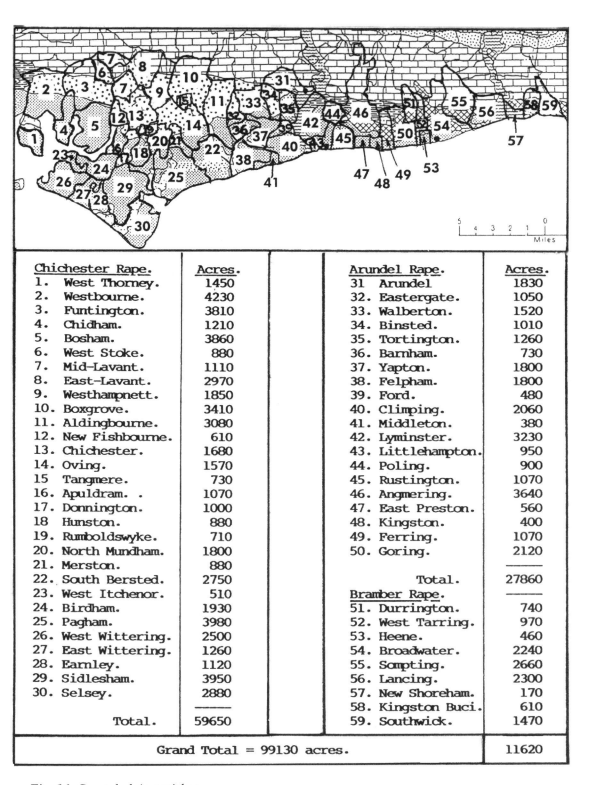

Chichester Rape.	Acres.		Arundel Rape.	Acres.
1. West Thorney.	1450		31. Arundel	1830
2. Westbourne.	4230		32. Eastergate.	1050
3. Funtington.	3810		33. Walberton.	1520
4. Chidham.	1210		34. Binsted.	1010
5. Bosham.	3860		35. Tortington.	1260
6. West Stoke.	880		36. Barnham.	730
7. Mid-Lavant.	1110		37. Yapton.	1800
8. East-Lavant.	2970		38. Felpham.	1800
9. Westhampnett.	1850		39. Ford.	480
10. Boxgrove.	3410		40. Climping.	2060
11. Aldingbourne.	3080		41. Middleton.	380
12. New Fishbourne.	610		42. Lyminster.	3230
13. Chichester.	1680		43. Littlehampton.	950
14. Oving.	1570		44. Poling.	900
15 Tangmere.	730		45. Rustington.	1070
16. Apuldram. .	1070		46. Angmering.	3640
17. Donnington.	1000		47. East Preston.	560
18 Hunston.	880		48. Kingston.	400
19. Rumboldswyke.	710		49. Ferring.	1070
20. North Mundham.	1800		50. Goring.	2120
21. Merston.	880			
22. South Bersted.	2750		Total.	27860
23. West Itchenor.	510		Bramber Rape.	
24. Birdham.	1930		51. Durrington.	740
25. Pagham.	3980		52. West Tarring.	970
26. West Wittering.	2500		53. Heene.	460
27. East Wittering.	1260		54. Broadwater.	2240
28. Earnley.	1120		55. Sompting.	2660
29. Sidlesham.	3950		56. Lancing.	2300
30. Selsey.	2880		57. New Shoreham.	170
			58. Kingston Buci.	610
Total.	59650		59. Southwick.	1470
Grand Total = 99130 acres.				11620

Fig. 16 *Coastal plain parishes*

the total of 3034 probate inventories relate to Broadwater parish, and only 48 of these [1.6% of the total] can be directly attributed to Worthing, the authors considered it essential that the probate inventories for the whole region were used for analysis, and not just those of Worthing and Broadwater, if the conclusions were to be meaningful.

As contemporary records suggest that income usually reflects an individual's status in the community,[37] it is not unreasonable to suggest that the 'Total Estate Value' [TEV] of the deceased's 'movable' or personal estate, as recorded in their probate inventory, not only reflected their income but also their status. Even though the categorisation of individuals into defined 'social groups' based solely on wealth remains both an emotive and controversial subject, the authors considered it would, nevertheless, form a suitable basis for determining 'notional' status. Using the concept of 'normal distribution', a 'statistical model' was therefore used to establish the following 'Notional Social Groups'.[38]

Group	TEV	Description of Group
1	Up to £5.00	Very Poor
2	£5.00 to £14.99	Poor
3	£15.00 to £49.99	Lower Middling
4	£50.00 to £199.99	Upper Middling
5	£200.00 to £554.99	Rich
6	Over £555.00	Very Rich

Within the total of 3034 probate inventories for the coastal plain region, one third specify the deceased's trade or occupation and the average TEV for each trade or occupational group was calculated and used to determine their status within the above social groups.

At the top of the social hierarchy were the very rich, often described simply as 'Gentlemen', even though the content of their probate inventories clearly show they were often involved in agricultural pursuits, albeit sometimes indirectly. By far the largest trade or occupational group [62%] were those directly involved in agriculture, namely 379 yeomen with an average TEV of £242.00 and 271 husbandmen with an average TEV of £59.00. While this places the average yeoman in Group 5 (Rich) and the average husbandman in Group 4 (Upper Middling) the range of individual TEVs for both yeoman and husbandman was quite wide. Individually a more wealthy husbandman could fall within Group 5 (Rich) while one of the poorer yeomen might well fall within Group 4 (Upper Middling). Indeed, there are several examples where an individual described himself as a yeoman when he made his will, but was described by his friends and neighbours as a husbandman when they prepared the probate inventory. Despite these limitations the yeoman and husbandman were nearly always near the top of the social hierarchy of the community in which they lived. In the lower social groups were the inhabitants who pursued other trades or occupations (often not recorded in the probate inventory) who also relied on agriculture in order to survive.

As arable land, pasture and meadow are seldom recorded in inventories, the computation of the total acreage for any individual farm is fraught with difficulties. According to one historian there was little if any fallow land in Sussex, as animal foodstuffs such as tares, vetches and pulse crops were grown in order to restore the land after the grain harvest.[39] However, the crops growing in the fields and the work carried out on the land are recorded, and from an analysis of the arable or cropped acreages the average size of arable holding for each of the social groups was calculated as follows.

Group	TEV	Average No. of Acres
3	£15.00 to £49.99	11
4	£50.00 to 199.99	37
5	£200.00 to 554.99	85
6	Over £550.00	242

The few examples of inventories with a TEV of less than £15.00 contained insuffi-cient data to form any real conclusions with regard to the size of arable holding. It would appear that people with a TEV below this value were invariably not self sufficient, and had to rely on either wages or poor relief to survive. For them deficient harvests and/or rising prices would have been catastrophic. All those in category 3 and above would have been above the subsistence level in a normal farming year devoid of plague, deficient harvests etc. Those higher up the social hierarchy were more insulated from higher prices and fluctuations in harvest yields, as they had either sufficient capital or stored grain to see them through the bad years.

Analysis of the crops grown on the 6,023 acres [2,438 hectares] recorded in the inventories for the 59 Coastal Plain parishes reveals that corn growing remained the economic basis of this prosperous region.[40] Wheat accounted for 37% of the crops grown, barley 28% and oats a poor third at 8%.[41] It would appear that oats were primarily used as animal feed, since a number of inventories record mixed crops of oats, peas and tares/vetches. The inventory of Thomas Gunn of Broadwater for example in 1681 records 66 acres of such crops (representing 26% of his total acreage), presumably grown to help feed his 1,400 animals.[42]

Over 15,000 animals are recorded in the Coastal Plain inventories, of which 69% were sheep, 15% cattle, 13% pigs and 3% horses.[43] These percentages, however, merely show the descending order of magnitude of the total number of animals recorded. Although each person had a modicum of choice as to what livestock they kept, their occupation, trade and social position were major factors in determining the type of animal and the quantity required. This is demonstrated by the number and type of animals recorded in the seventeenth-century inventories of Worthing inhabitants in each of the four following social groups.

Social Group		Name	Date	Sheep	Cattle	Pigs	Horses	TOTAL
2	Poor	David Symonds	1671	3 [100%]	-			3
3	Lower Middling	Joan Swift	1640	4 [40%]	4 [40%]	2 [20%]		10
4	Upper Middling	John Stempe	1624	24[64%]	5 [14%]	4 [14%]	3 [8%]	37
5	Rich	Thos. Campion	1647	238[83%]	19[7%]	27 [9%]	3 [1%]	287

Corn was produced using sheep corn husbandry, compelemented with some fattening of stock or dairy farming, typical of most 'mixed' farming areas. With the exception of that grown by those living below or at subsistence level, most of the corn was grown for profit and, if not sold privately, was sold at market. Although Broadwater was still considered to be a market town in 1637, its survival was precarious, for it was being overshadowed by the growing importance of the adjacent market at West Tarring, which was described in 1568 as one of the major corn markets in the country.[44] However, by far the largest corn and cattle market in the area was held at Chichester, which served a large hinterland. During the early part of the seventeenth century, wheat was exported from the port at Chichester to the Low Countries, and between 1650–1652 Chichester was regularly providing 1,000 quarters of wheat and 1,500 quarters of malt as provisions for the Cromwellian armies. It has even been suggested that from the middle of the seventeenth century 'nearly every ship that left the port of Chichester carried a cargo of corn'.[45]

From the information contained in probate inventories certain deductions and obser-vations can also be made about the pre-nineteenth-century houses in the hamlet of Worthing. It has been suggested that the order in which rooms were recorded represented the route that the assessor(s) took through the house when identifying and valuing the contents of the various rooms. Some historians have used this assumption to compare the extracted information relating to the various rooms, with actual examples of surviving houses of known dates, to establish the evolution of basic house plans.[46]

Although this type of in depth study for a whole region is far beyond the scope of this book, the information contained solely in the Worthing probate inventories is sufficient to reveal the various types of houses that were constructed in the hamlet. Between 1570 and 1640 large sections of the rural community had, for the first time, both the security of tenure and sufficient spare capital to invest in the erection of relatively expensive buildings of permanent materials. The evidence of the 'Great Rebuilding' throughout most of England during this period possibly explains why many of the wealthier inhabitants rebuilt, reconstructed or extended their houses.[47] Most seventeenth-century buildings which survive result from this 'Great Rebuilding', which was responsible for the destruction of many of the former medieval houses. It is perhaps fortunate that the changes that did occur are often reflected in surviving probate inventories, even though the exact location of the recorded house remains unidentified.

Many of those people at the lower end of the social scale still resided in late medieval houses, and the Worthing inventory of Joan Swift (dated 1640)[48] reveals a typical example. This single-storey building, where a chamber was divided from the hall, probably by means of a partition, contained an open hearth situated in the hall, possibly near an end wall. In this type of house the smoke emanating from the hearth tended to fill the house before finally escaping from a hole in the roof or beneath the eaves. In these early houses with open hearths extra space was achieved by constructing wooden platforms at first floor level at each end of the house if required, and 'Bayleaf farmstead' reconstructed at the Weald and Downland Museum at Singleton is a 'living' example. These platforms, known as 'lofts', were accessible by ladders and were initially used for storage, but gradually became used for additional sleeping accommodation. The inventory of Thomas Kinge of Worthing (dated 1637) records a similar house to that previously described, but with the addition of a 'Lofte over the Hall' and 'Lofte over the chamber'.[49]

The smoke-filled environment of these early buildings was improved considerably when bricks became more generally available and chimneys were built to vent the smoke. At first the chimneys were added to the end(s) of the houses but by the early seventeenth century they were being sited centrally in the house to provide back-to-back heat to two rooms at the same time. This enabled a first floor accessed by a staircase to be incorporated which provided additional living space for the larger families, and of course, more fire places which gradually became a status symbol. There are numerous examples of chambers at first floor level in the later seventeenth-century probate inventories. A typical example at Worthing is the probate inventory dated 1685 for a yeoman named Henry English, in which is recorded a kitchen, hall and parlour, with a chamber over each of them.[50] All the rooms upstairs were now furnished as bedrooms, as it was no longer fashionable to sleep in a chamber on the ground floor, and the modern practice of sleeping at first floor level was established.[51]

It has been recorded that, due to the chimney becoming a symbol of status, several Tudor houses possessed more chimneys than rooms![52] With the advent of more and more chimneys in houses during the seventeenth century it did not take a genius to recognise it as a potentially lucrative source of revenue for the Crown. Consequently a 'Hearth Tax' was levied in 1662 to help raise money for King Charles II after his restoration, and occupiers of houses (rather than owners) were taxed two shillings [10p] for each hearth in their property. This tax was collected in two instalments : viz. Ladyday (25th March) and Michaelmas (29th September). Those persons in receipt of poor relief or occupying houses valued at less than 20 shillings [£1] per annum were exempt. (On the Worthing Hearth Tax lists these are marked 'Ex'.) This tax was levied from 1662 to 1689, when it was repealed and eventually replaced by the 'Land Tax', which was collected from 1692 to 1831, and the 'Window Tax' in 1696 (implemented to help meet the cost of re-minting England's damaged coinage).[53]

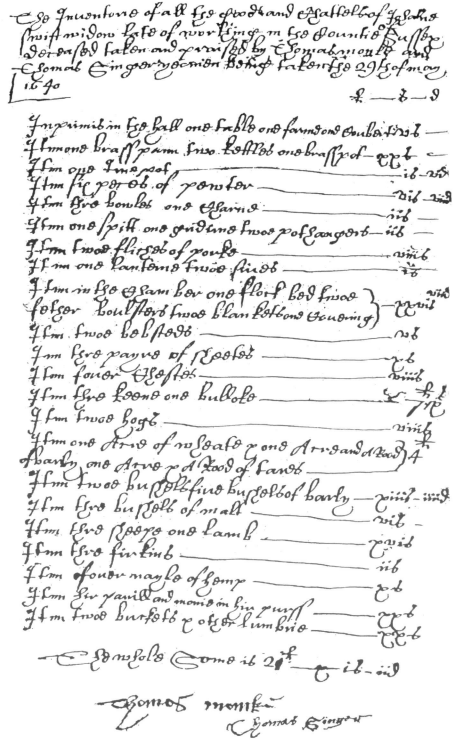

Fig. 17 Probate of Joan Swift (1640)

The Hearth Tax Lists provide the earliest record of both the houses and their occupiers for the hamlet of Worthing. Reproduced below is the list for 1664 and 1665.

Hearth Tax Lists for Worthing in 1664 and 1665

	Occupier in 1664		No. of Hearths	Occupier in 1665	House no. on Fig. 19
1	John Easton		2	Henry Stoneham	
2	Douglas Easton	(Ex)	5	Douglas Easton	
3	Richard Hune		3	John Ireland	37
4	William Deane		1	William Deane	
5	Mary King, widow		2	Edward Humphrey	
6	Joane Monke, widow	(Ex)	2	Joane Monke, widow	
7	William Cheeseman, sen.		1	James Lock	
8	William Cheeseman, jun.	(Ex)	2	William Cheeseman, jun.	
9	John Newman		1	David Symonds	11
10	Phillipp Stamer	(Ex)	3	Phillip Stamer	6
11	William Monke	(Ex)	3	William Monke	
12	John Stempe, sen.	(Ex) *	2	—	
13	Thomas Monke, sen.	(Ex)	3	Thomas Monke, sen.	
14	Thomas Monke, jun.	(Ex)	4	Thomas Monke, jun.	
				Bennet Monke	
15	Richard Singer	(Ex)	2	Richard Singer	
16	Henry Gilbert		2	Henry Gilbert	
17	John Roach	(Ex)	1	John Roach	
18	Richard Elmes	(Ex)	1	Richard Elmes	
19	Edward Hide		2	John Newman	1
20	Henry Stoneham		2	Simon Humfree & Widow Mose *	
21	Overington Wood		2	Overington Wood	
22	Thomas French	(Ex)	2	Thomas French	
23	Richard Hardham		1	Richard Hardham	
24	John Harwood		3	William Harwood	
25	Edward Humphrey		1	William Deane	
26	John Stempe, jun.		1	Widow Jollife	
27	Henry English	(Ex)	2	Henry English	
28	John Cobb	(Ex)	2	John Cobb	
29	John Stoneham	(Ex)	1	John Stoneham	32
30	Richard Easton	(Ex)	2	Richard Easton	
31	Peter Price		1	Peter Price	
32	Nevill Hersey		3	William Harwood	
33	William Harwood		1	Thomas Cooper	
34	George Symes		2	Thomas Harwood	
35	Jeoffrey Hoodlasse		1	Jeoffrey Hoodlasse	
36	Thomas Martine	(Ex)	1	Thomas Martine	
37	Thomas Cooper	(Ex)	1	Thomas Cooper	
38	William Martine		1	William Martine	
39	Widow Jolliffe		1	Thomas Monke, sen.	
40	Tilsey		3	Thomas Monke, sen., the land	

(Ex)= Exonerated payment   *= described as 'poor or 'very poor'

While these documents help determine the number of houses that existed at Worthing at that time, they have only limited use, for they do not provide any positive information on the actual location of the houses listed. Some historians have suggested that the lists were

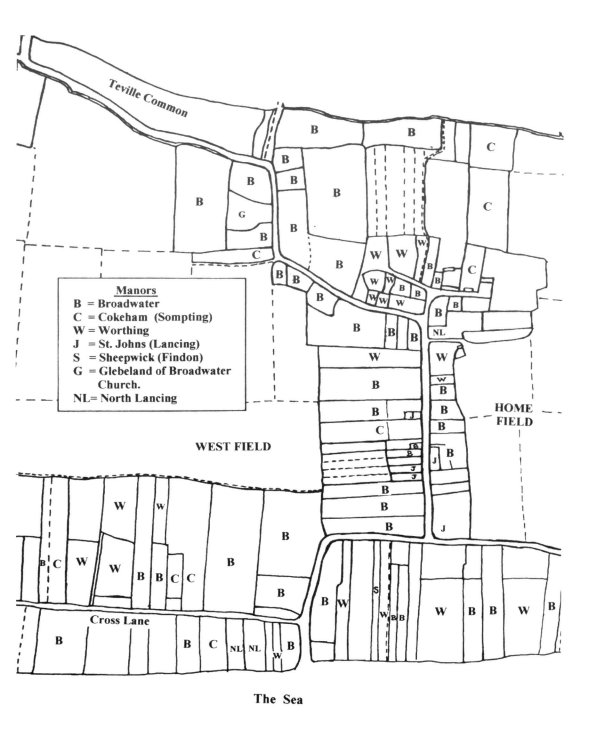

Fig. 18 *Manorial ownership of the old enclosures*

compiled in a logical manner, such as walking order, but at Worthing there are unfortunately no clues as to the starting point of the assessor.

Although it is apparent that, prior to the Inclosure Act of 1805, the majority of the
houses and cottages in the hamlet of Worthing were all erected on the old enclosures or
plots of land that were clustered either side of Worthing Street and Cross Lane, the task of
identifying their exact location is beset with problems. As many of these early buildings did
not survive until the publication of the first reasonably detailed map of Worthing in 1814,[54]
one has to rely on other documentary sources in which buildings may be referred to or
recorded. These again rarely provide clues as to the properties' location. When boundaries
of the property are described, these are invariably for the piece of land or site on which the
building had been erected. Detailed descriptions, and the date the house or cottage was
built, are also rarely given. Even the probate inventories at best only record the number of
rooms together with a description of the goods and chattels in each room. Only in two or
three instances have buildings survived long enough for photographic evidence to be
available. Even engravings only record the more prominent and picturesque large buildings
of the emerging town of Worthing.

The problem at Worthing is exacerbated because the land tenure was under the
jurisdiction of at least six separate manors. By far the largest were Broadwater and
Worthing, the remainder being Lancing (the ancient manor of St. Johns), Cokeham (in
Sompting), North Lancing and Monks and Sheepwick (Findon). Moreover, the land was not
equally divided between these manors, or in any perceptible pattern, and ranged from a few
hundred acres held under Broadwater manor to a solitary one-acre strip held from Sheepwick manor. Consequently each of the appropriate manorial court books, in conjunction
with other sources, had to be researched in order to obtain any relevant information, and to
identify the location of the various houses and their sites. The manorial ownership of each
of the old enclosures and plots of land on Figure 18 have, wherever possible, been
identified with a letter denoting their respective manors. At the time of writing the manorial
jurisdiction for a few of the plots remains unidentified, and accordingly these have been left
blank.

The lifestyle of the vast majority of Worthing's seventeenth-century inhabitants was
still dictated and controlled by the lord of the manor. Each owed allegiance, labour services
and/or rents, the amount or type dependent on the inhabitant's status within the manor.
Under this old feudal system (which was finally abolished by Statute in 1660) manorial
courts were required to be held twice a year: but in practice they were often only held
annually. Transactions concerning the transfer of tenants to and from properties in a
particular manor were recorded in the manorial court rolls (which later continued in books).
The earliest surviving court books are for Worthing manor which commence in 1544, when
the medieval obligations or services required of the tenants by the lord of the manor had
been converted to cash payments and annual rental payments. By the sixteenth century the
means of holding land from the lord of the manor was either 'free' or 'customary' (held at
the will of the lord according to the customs of the manor). Freehold land was subject to the
common law of the land while 'customary' (servile) tenants, were, as the name implies,
subject only to the customs of the manor, and these tenants could not appeal to common law
to resolve any problems of land tenure.

Originally there were three manorial courts held, often, but not necessarily, on the
same day. The 'Court Baron' related to the freeholders while the 'Court Customary' was for
the customary tenants. A 'Court Leet' dealt with minor criminal offences which were
punished by confinement in the local stocks or pillory, or a small monetary payment to the
court. By at least the seventeenth century the Courts Baron and Customary had been
combined at Broadwater manor under the heading of 'Court Baron' while the 'Court Leet'

was often held at the end of the 'Court Baron', but recorded separately. At Broadwater this dealt mainly with repairs to buildings and fences, scouring of ditches and watercourses and matters concerning the pound where wandering animals were secured. The court proceedings were generally recorded in Latin up to 1734, thereafter they were written in English.[55] The majority of the tenants recorded in the manorial court books are 'customary' and, since the only title that they had to their property was a copy on parchment of their entry in the court book, these tenants were referred to as 'copyholders'.

There is a certain amount of jargon used in the manorial court books and the following explanation is included to provide an understanding of any manorial court extracts used later when describing the various properties. When a 'copyholder' went into a property, he was said to be 'admitted' and the acceptance of this was recorded in the manorial court books. Conversely to relinquish a property it had to be 'surrendered' to the use of the lord of the manor by the outgoing tenant before the next tenant could be admitted. A 'fine' (payment) was made to the lord by the incoming tenant. On the death of a tenant a 'heriot' was required, which was a payment in kind and usually the 'best animal or beast' of the deceased. If the deceased's heir was unwilling to pass over the heriot it was forcibly seized by either the steward or another official of the lord of the manor. The custom of 'Borough English' applied to most, if not all, the manors encountered at Worthing. This is where the youngest son inherited the property and not the eldest as in 'primogeniture'. If there were no sons the youngest daughter inherited. Technically copyholders' property could not be inherited unless it had been previously recorded in court as 'surrendered to the use of the tenant's will', whereas freeholders could leave their land directly to their heirs.

No great houses, occupied by people of national importance such as royalty or nobility, have been found in the hamlet of Worthing during the authors' research for this book. Only smaller houses occupied by the tenant farmers (yeomen and husbandmen), tradesmen and fishermen etc. were found. These were the 'human backbone of the nation' and their dwelling houses fall within the group of buildings that are today described as 'domestic vernacular architecture'.[56] It should however be noted that the period houses today described as 'cottages' are not those that belonged to the poor, but were probably the former houses of the wealthy yeomen.[57]

The conjectural map reproduced as Fig. 19 on page 47 is derived from the evidence contained in all the documents researched and shows those sites in the hamlet of Worthing on which houses have been identified for the period 1544 to 1780. Each of the houses on this map is marked by a number within a circle, for ease of identification. It must not, however, be assumed that all the sites contained houses continuously throughout the whole period. Indeed several of the houses that existed in the seventeenth century did not survive until the next century, while others were not erected until the eighteenth century. It is for this reason a table of brief historical notes for each of the sites has been inserted on the page opposite Figure 19.

The majority of the houses were identified from the manorial court books of Broadwater, Worthing and Lancing, but only a few can be attributed directly to names in the 'Hearth Tax' lists. This is partly due to tenants sub-letting their properties, since the resulting under-tenants are rarely mentioned in these court books. It is also due to the large time-gap between the Hearth Tax lists of the 1664/5 and the first positive identifiable entries in the surviving court books of Broadwater in the 1690's and Lancing (the old manor of St. John's) in the 1770's. However, the few properties that have been 'matched-up' have been marked accordingly on the Hearth Tax lists on page 42 with the appropriate number on Figure 19. It is hoped that future research might produce some more.

In a book like this, which is endeavouring to reconstruct a chronology of Worthing's earlier history, it is not possible to reconstruct the detailed history of every identifiable

Brief Historical Notes for Each of the Sites

The following convention has been used in the table:-

The earliest recorded occupant and date is shown first together with any relevant notes in brackets. Names in inverted commas are those most commonly used in the records to describe the property.

R = property rebuilt (or a new house erected) on or between the dates shown.

D = property demolished on or between dates shown.

CS = current situation (AD2000) and specifies properties currently on site.

An asterisk * against the site number denotes that the property is considered in more depth in the subsequent text.

Brief historical notes of sites as numbered on Figure 19

1. John Newman, 1715; R 1803-21 Robinson's house and wagon office; CS Portland Buildings.
2. Henry Monk, 1682; R 1793 Worthing House; CS Blockbuster Video.
3. Thomas Upperton, 1690; D 1814-38?; CS Part of old Davison School and car park.
4*. John Monke, 1687; R 1807-11 Wortley House; D 1986 - for road widening.
5. Edward Hoar, 1743; R 1881-96 Campion Terrace; D 1986 - for road widening.
6*. Catherine Stammer, 1637 Stammers; R 1793-1814 Thurloe House; D c.1959; CS Police Station and part of car park.
7. John Newland, 1806 'part of Tobees'; D 1958-67 CS Car Park.
8. Ingram Lingoe, 1736 - later John Hickox; D by 1970; CS Multi Storey Car Park Ann Street.
9. James Denyer, 1778 Campions; D by 1970; CS Multi Storey Car Park Ann Street.
10. Rev. William Wade, 1699 'part of his Estate'; D by 1810; CS Bunce & Co.
11. David Symmons, 1671; D by 1780; CS Site destroyed by road widening in 1986.
12*. Nicholas Page, 1596 Manor of Raymonds; D 1847 The Farm; CS Citizens' Advice Bureau.
13*. John Smith, 1544 ('Dukes'); D1737-80; CS Part of site destroyed by road widening in 1986.
14*. Thomas Lamball, 1551 Sawoods; D1714-1747; CS Part of site destroyed by road widening in 1986.
15*. Thomas Lambell, 1551 Lambolds; D 1912-1943; CS Part of site destroyed by road widening in 1986.
16*. Ferdinando Lindup, 1700; R possibly by c.1754 - the Swan Inn by c.1849; CS House still on this site.
17.   ?   , c. 1790 (but probably much earlier) Box Cottage; CS House still on site.
18. Possibly Richard Elmes, 1679; R by 1800 as North End Cottage/ The Hollies: CS House still standing.
19. Possibly John Furzeman, 1762; D 1880-96; CS Upper High Street covers this site.
20. Possibly Ann Swift, 1671; D before 1786; CS Former scrap metal yard on this site.
21 Thomas Redford by 1791, D 1943- 68; CS Wicker House complex covers this site.
22. John Marley,1804 The Anchor; R c, 1895; CS Re-named The Jack Horner 1989.
23*. Alex. Burden, 1762; D 1960 - for road improvements; CS Safeways superstore.
24*. Edward Stamer, 1551 - later Alma Cottage; D 1948; CS Safeways superstore.
25*. Thomas Campion, 1667 Cookes; D 1960's? - former Manor House; CS Safeways superstore.
26*. John Stempe, 1624 - later Sherwoods and Brapples; D 1822; CS Scout Hall on this site.
27*. Thomas King, 1690 - later Corfes; R at some stage as The Toby Jug; CS House still on site.
28*. Henry Allen, 1711 Giles; R in 19thC as a Boys' School - later Orchard House; D in the 1970s; CS Crown House on this site.
29*. John Mitchell, 1778; D 1821-1838; CS Crown House on this site.
30*. Thomas Mitchell, 1778; R possibly at some stage?; CS House still on this site.
31. William Greenyer, 1651 - later Campions; D 1786-1801; CS Buildings on N. side of Elm Rd.
32. Michael Wheateleye, 1645 - later Stonehams and Sopers; D prior to 1778 Warwick House built on its site; CS Broadway Mansions.
33 Thomas Campion, 1692 - later Badgers Buildings; D1880-96; CS Steyne Methodist Church.
34 & 35. Richard Stubbs purchased from John Newland prior to 1801; D c.1801; CS Northern end of Steyne Gardens.
36. John Cooper, 1631; R c. 1790 as Lane's House - later Bedford House; D 1940; CS Bus Depot and 18 Warwick Street.
37*. Nicholas Page, 1597 South House and lands; D c.1790; CS 10-16 Warwick Street and Bedford Row to the sea front.
38. 17th Century house mentioned in old deeds- no further details; CS Grafton Multi Storey Car Park.
39. Simon Campion, 1661 Dawtreys; D by 1746; CS 82-94 Montague Street.

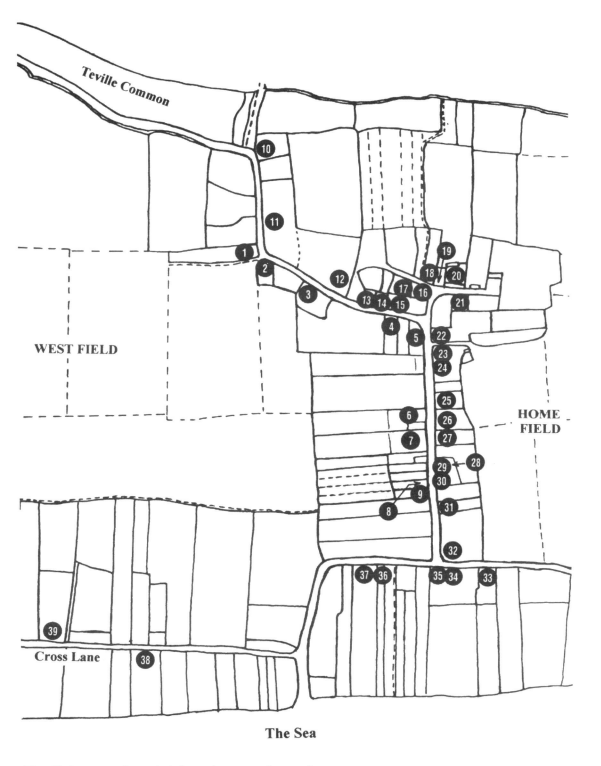

Fig. 19 *Seventeenth- and eighteenth-century house sites*

property. Some of the oldest and most interesting sites together with the properties constructed on them have, therefore, been selected for further and more detailed consideration.

As anticipated, some of the earliest properties in Worthing are located in and around North Street and the top of High Street, near the original Saxon settlement. The property marked 12 on Fig. 20 was built on freehold land of the manor of Broadwater. All the available evidence indicates that it was part of the reputed ancient manor of 'Raymonds'

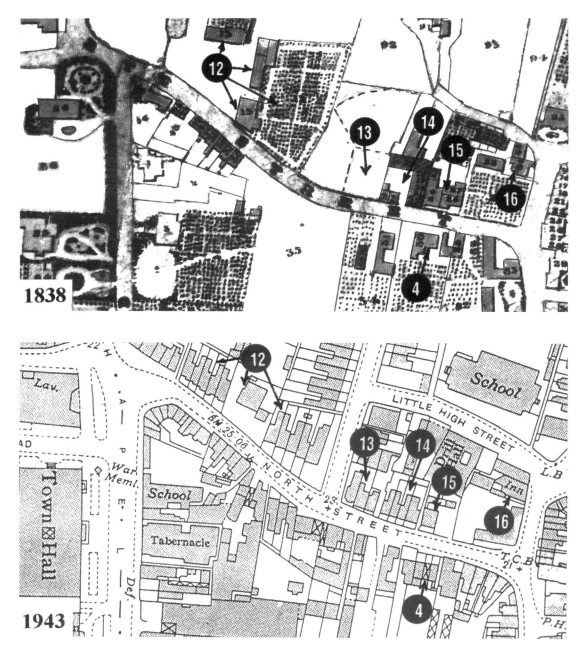

Fig. 20 Maps of North Street, 1838 and 1943

which may have derived its name from the Raymond family which held lands in Worthing from the fifteenth century.[58] This manor has been traced from 1596, when it was held by Nicholas Page and his wife Anne, until 1780 when it was acquired by William Markes.[59] Further details of this manor have now been found. A house undoubtedly stood on this site for a very long time for at the death of Nicholas Page in 1634 the property was described as the 'manor and capital messuage of "Raymonds" in Worthing' (a 'capital messuage' being a substantial house). In 1752 the land tax records this property as 'The Farm', owned by Mr. Ferris and occupied by R. Lindup, while in later deeds the site of 1.5 acres [0.61 hectares] is described as containing a 'messuage' (house), barn and other buildings.[60] The 1814 map shows several buildings on the site which presumably included the barn and a house, possibly that of 1634. In April 1822 the property was purchased for £700 by Thomas Fuller, a coachmaker of Worthing, from William Westbrooke Richardson who had inherited it from his father Thomas Richardson Esq. From deeds it appears that the buildings may have been in disrepair and very old since it is recorded that Thomas Fuller intended to build a substantial new house on the site. He mortgaged the property to obtain money for that purpose between 1822 and 1828. By 1832 Fuller had not repaid the mortgage by the agreed dates and the property was sold by public auction when it was purchased by Mr. George A. Muskett of Bermondsey, one of the mortgagees. It would appear that no new buildings had been erected by Fuller and all the old building had been demolished by the time Harry Newland purchased the site in 1847 following Muscketts death. This site was then sub-divided into three separate gardens which adjoined Mr. Harry Newland's new house (Worthing Lodge) that had been built immediately to the west in 1846. After Harry Newland's death in 1857 the gardens were sold off, and between c. 1885 and 1906 numbers 1 to 23 North Street were built.

Fig. 21 *Numbers 1-23 North Street*

    All the houses except the central one were eventually purchased by Worthing Borough Council and demolished to make way for road widening in 1986. The central house still survives and is owned by West Sussex County Council, but as a result of the

Fig 22 Montpelier Villa (today the Citizen's Advice Bureau)

road widening on its southern side the new carriageway of North Street now passes closer to the front door of this house and the remains of its former front lawn and garden have been made into a car park.

Further to the east, on the same side of the street, were three old copyhold enclosures of Worthing manor adjacent to each other. The first property, marked 13 on Fig. 20, was recorded in 1544 as 'A cottage and virgate of land formerly Dukes'. The virgate of land was about 14 acres spread among the open fields and the messuage (cottage or house) was located on one rood of land [0.25 acre] facing Worthing Street (now North Street). Members of the Duke family are recorded in the parish from the fourteenth century. Very little is known about the cottage other than it descended through the families of Smith, Searle and Monk during the sixteenth and seventeenth centuries before being amalgamated into the Rev. Wade's estate in c. 1701. It was acquired by John Booker of Arundel in 1702 and finally passed to Charles Bushby, also of Arundel, a mercer, in 1771. The cottage is not shown on Phillip's map of 1814 and it is thought that it had gone prior to 1780. No further development took place on this site until 1880 when the 'British Land Company' acquired the property as part of their 'South Downs Park' estate and divided it into building plots, three fronting North Street and others on the east side of a new roadway called Ashdown Road. Directories record that the three houses, numbered 25 to 29 North Street, were erected and occupied between c. 1882 and 1887. When workmen were excavating for the foundations, the builder Mr. G. C. Parsons reported that they came upon the base of an old wall which was believed to be the site of the old chapel of Worthing (recorded from 1291).[61] This now seems unlikely as it would make more sense to suggest that they uncovered part of the foundation of the former cottage. These three houses survived until 1986 when they were demolished to make way for road widening.

Fig. 23 *Numbers 25-37 North Street*

To the east of this property on an enclosure of one rood (0.25 acre) was a property (marked 14 on Fig. 23) which was recorded as 'A cottage and one acre of land called Sawoods' in the manorial court books of Worthing in 1551. The property descended through the families of Lamball, Blackman and Geering until 14th October 1661 when it passed to Richard Hardham. The Hearth Tax of 1664 lists Hardham as occupying a dwelling house with one hearth, suggesting a small and possibly ancient cottage. Hardham, however, died by 1670 and his youngest daughter, Elizabeth Dyer (wife of James Dyer), was admitted to the property. By 1714 she had also died and there was a gap of some 33 years before the next occupant. During this time it appears that the cottage either fell into ruins or was demolished. By 1747 it is described as only a 'toft and parcel of land containing one rood'. By 1810 Edward Penfold had acquired the property and a barn is shown at the north end of the site on the 1814 map. The Hide survey of 1838 shows eight houses built around the perimeter of the site with stables (the old barn). These houses still survived in 1898 but had been replaced with a terrace of four houses by the time that the 1912 Ordnance Survey map had been published. This terrace was also demolished in 1986 for road widening.

To the east of the previous property was another copyhold piece of Worthing manor, (marked 15 on Fig. 23) which was recorded in 1551 as part of 'one messuage and a virgate of land called Lambolds'. Members of the Lamball family (spelt as Lamvale, Lambold, Lambell etc.) occur numerous times in the Parish Registers from the fourteenth century. Since the cottage is later recorded on a site together with an adjoining garden, the property may possibly be the same as that belonging to Thomas and Lucy Lamvale between 1396 and 1438, recorded as 'a messuage with garden and 2 acres of land in Wordhyng'.[62] The property then descended through the Lamball, Blackman, Geering and Buckeridge families

Fig. 24 *Lambold's farmhouse*

until 1755 when it was passed to John Penfold, yeoman of Broadwater. In 1785 it was acquired by Richard Bacon, a fisherman of Worthing, and by 1810 Bacon had built two other houses adjoining his own house (see Fig. 20). He let the eastern house to his son-in-law, George White, and the other to Thomas Artlett, also a fisherman. The houses were still shown on the 1912 Ordnance Survey map but by 1943 the two eastern ones had been demolished. The garden to the east later became 'Adcock's Garage' and this was demolished in 1959. The remaining house was demolished and part of the site was engulfed by road widening in 1986. A block of flats was constructed on the remainder of the site to the west and the garden on the east is now a small public open space.

To the north of this open space was an old freehold enclosure of Broadwater manor on which currently stands 'The Swan' public house (marked 16 on Fig. 20). By the end of the seventeenth century an earlier house of Ferdinando Lindup, a yeoman, stood on the site. At his death in 1780 his property is described in the manorial court books of Broadwater as a 'Messuage, Barn and 25 acres of land'. Although his probate inventory survives it is badly damaged, consequently very little information can be obtained concerning the house and its contents.[63] The property then passed to his son Thomas, whose marriage to Elizabeth Penfold of Heene produced no children. When he died in 1749, because all his brothers were already dead, the property was inherited by his nephew Richard Lindup, who was also a yeoman of Worthing. It is not known when the old house was demolished and the present one built but it is probable that it may have been erected just prior to Richard Lindup's marriage to Jenny Burden in 1754. It is recorded that the new building was originally 'a private house of Mr Richard Lindup', although this could equally well have referred to Richard Lindup's son, also Richard, who inherited the property in the latter part of the eighteenth century. In 1842 the building was described as a lodging house and by 1849 an Inn.[64] When 'The Swan' was enlarged and modernised in 1938, four brass medals commemorating the life and death of Princess Charlotte were found in a wall being demolished at the rear of the property. They were given to Worthing Museum. Princess Charlotte had stayed at Warwick House in 1807 when she visited Worthing.[65]

On the south side of North Street, near its junction with High Street, was a copyhold enclosure of Broadwater manor (marked 4 on Fig. 20). In the latter part of the seventeenth century this property was described as a 'messuage, barn, orchard and 8 acres' and was occupied by John Monke, a yeoman, his wife Joan and their three children. John Monke's probate inventory taken following his death in 1687 shows that the house on the site contained a hall, kitchen and parlour with a chamber over each. In the yard was a milkhouse and in the fields were his 37 farm animals which included 5 horses, 7 cattle, 17 sheep and 8 pigs. Stored in his barn was a total of 18 quarters of wheat, barley tares and oats. Although the property only included eight acres of land his inventory shows he was cultivating 23 acres -the extra acreage was presumably rented from elsewhere. His farm equipment included a plough, four harrows, a waggon, dung-cart, harness and winnowing tools, which were typical for a yeoman of this period. In 1687 the property passed to Thomas Monke, his cousin. In 1692 it was surrendered to the use of Anne Cowley and it then descended through the Cowley family until 1749 when Charles Tribe, a yeoman of Broadwater, acquired it. However in 1760 he surrendered it to Richard Lindup for the sum of £220. After Lindup's death in 1765 the property passed to his widow Jenny and then to their son, also Richard, in 1781. At some time between 1807 and 1811 it appears that the house was rebuilt and named Wortley House when it was described as 'Miss Phillip's and Gilmore's Seminary for Young Ladies at Wortley House'.[66] This rebuilding is confirmed when Richard Lindup's death was presented at the manorial court in 1835, for the property was

Fig. 25 The Swan Public House

Fig. 26 *Wortley House (with modern shopfronts in foreground)*

described as

> 'All that messuage, coachhouse, stable, garden and premises in the occupation of William Whitter, Gentleman, situate in Worthing and **formerly** consisting of a messuage, barn porch, gateroom, orchard and backside.'

After the death of Jane Lindup (Richard's widow) in 1852, their son-in-law George Newland inherited all the copyhold and freehold land of Richard and Jane Lindup. From *c.* 1850 to 1887 the house was used by a succession of tutors and school teachers as a school, with names such as 'Wortley House Academy' (1871) and 'Wortley House Young Ladies School' (1882-87). By 1891 an additional house had been erected adjoining the property on the west named 'La Venia'.

After the Second World War small one-storey shops were added to the front of Wortley House (see Fig. 26 above). The name Wortley House gradually fell into disuse and the building was converted into flats. The properties survived until 1986 when road widening was responsible for their demolition and the south carriageway of North Street now passes over their site.

The next group of buildings to be considered existed on either side of High Street. About half way down on the west side of the street was Stammer's Farm (marked 6 on Fig. 27), which was built on a copyhold enclosure of Broadwater manor. Its first positive identification is in 1637 when, as the name suggests, it was owned and occupied by the Stammer family, a surname that can be traced back at Worthing to the subsidy lists of 1327, 1379 and 1524/5.[67] This undoubtedly ancient property is described in Broadwater's manorial court books as 'all that messuage or tenement, two barns, stables, building and a piece of land behind the same estimated at one acre', together with twelve acres in the open fields. In 1637 Catherine Stammer, widow, died and the property passed to her son and heir John and thereafter through a further three generations of the Stammer family. Although no illustrations of this early property have been found, information from the probate inventories of Catherine Stammer and Phillip Stammer indicate that this farmhouse had a hall, buttery, milkhouse and a kitchen with a chamber (bedroom) above the kitchen.[68] John Stammer, the son of Catherine, who died in 1648, is recorded in the Protestation Returns of

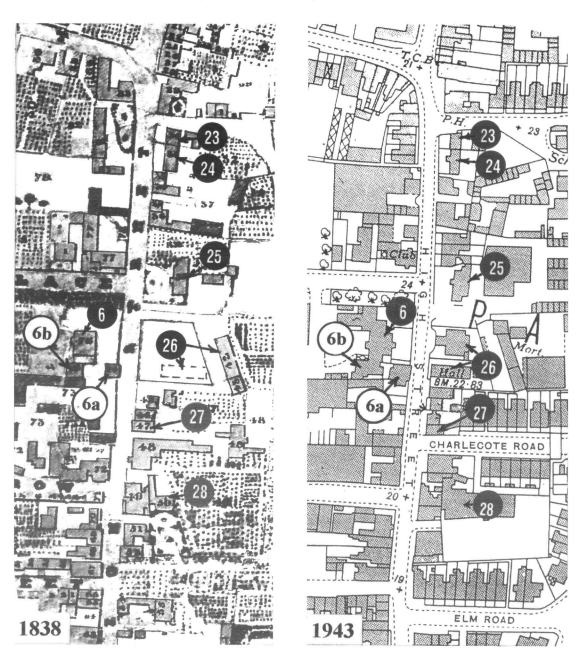

Fig 27 Maps of High Street, 1838 and 1943

1641, while his son Phillip (buried in 1670) is recorded on the Hearth Tax lists of 1664 and 1665 as occupying a house with 3 hearths.[70] The probate inventory of Phillip Stammer, prepared following his death in 1670, reveals that in addition to his own twelve acres he was also using a further 23 acres on two other farms in Worthing. His cultivated crops were almost equally divided between wheat, barley and tares (animal feed).

By the early part of the eighteenth century it appears that the Stammer family no longer resided in this property since in 1713, when Sarah Newland acquired the property from William Stammer, it was occupied by William Hamper. Sarah Newland was the widow of Richard Newland (died 1712) and the daughter of Henry Monk and in 1735 passed the property to her son and heir, Richard Newland. By then the farm's cultivated land had risen to an estimated eighteen acres. John Newland, son and heir of Richard, was admitted to the property after his father's death in 1757 and later in 1793 it became freehold when John Newland purchased the manor of Broadwater. Although the exact location of the old farmhouse cannot be determined from the small-scale map of Yeakell and Gardner of *c.*1780, the building shown on Phillip's map of Worthing dated 1814 may well be the same house. Later photographs show the rear of the house to be old despite the fact that the front appears to be of Georgian or even Victorian origin. It appears therefore that the original old farmhouse was either given a new facade prior to the 1850's or was demolished to make way for a new house built between *c.* 1793 and 1814, perhaps by George Newland, son and one of the heirs of John Newland, after his father's death in 1806. This house was later known as Thurloe House and was occupied by John Wakefield, a magistrate, for several years and after his death, by William Tribe who moved there from Warwick Street.[71]

To the south of Thurloe House was a small piece of land, held of the manor of Lancing, which in the court book for 1778 was described as 'A building called a carthouse

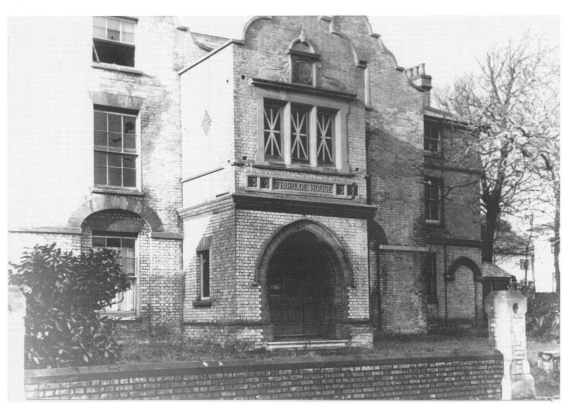

Fig. 28 Thurloe House

Fig. 29 *Old cottage near Thurloe House*

(now fell down) and one Rood of copyhold land with the appurtenances in Worthing' held by Phillip Stammer, deceased.[72] Despite several court requests for Phillip's son and heir to come and claim the property he failed to do so and it was formally seized on the 10th December 1778 by the Bailiff of the manor of Lancing, Thomas Burden, who lived nearby on the opposite side of High Street. William Badger, a fisherman of Worthing, and his wife Ruth immediately acquired the property and by 1782 when it was sold to Jane Snook of Broadwater, had built a cottage on it, which adjoined the street. It was described as a 'new erected copyhold or customary messuage or tenement' and is marked 6a on Fig 27. An illustration of this cottage is reproduced as Fig. 29 and is described by D. R. Elleray as 'A fine eighteenth-century mansard cottage in cobble flint with yellow brick dressings'.[73]

In 1807 George Wingfield, the younger, was admitted to the property and within three years had built a second cottage to the rear of the first one and adjacent to Thurloe House. This second cottage was later known as Smugglers House[74] (marked 6b on Fig 30). Unfortunately George Wingfield was later declared a bankrupt and all his property was sold by public auction in February 1824. The two cottages were purchased by John Wakefield who, by then, occupied Thurloe House next door. He subsequently mortgaged the property to William Tribe in 1830 and after his death in 1832 William Tribe was admitted on default of a payment by Wakefield. On the 28th November 1879 the property became freehold by a deed of enfranchisement by the manor of Lancing and thereafter the cottages became an integral part of the Thurloe House property. The combined property descended through the Tribe family and was purchased by the West Sussex County Council on 25th May 1921: by 1922/3 Thurloe House had become the County Police Central Station and remained as such until the present Police Station was built in Union Place in 1939.[75] The current Police Station and part of a car park in High Street now cover the site of the old properties.

The present Safeways supermarket premises on the corner of Lyndhurst Road and High Street are located on the former sites of two ancient properties. The property on the first site, marked 24 on Fig. 27, was a copyhold parcel of land of Worthing manor. It can be traced back to 1551 when it is recorded as 'a cottage and garden and 2 Hemplotts formerly Lamballes'. The tenant was Edward Stamer. The property descended through the Stamer family until 1666, when Elizabeth Stamer surrendered it and her sister, Joane Swift, was admitted. When the property was surrendered it was described as 'a cottage and garden and 2 Hemplotts estimated as 1 acre'. Elizabeth Swift, daughter of John Swift of Lancing, was the next person to be admitted to the property. The cottage was, however, described as 'ruinous'.

The next entry relating to the property was in 1686, some 20 years later when an Elizabeth Burden surrendered the property to her children Mary and Peter Burden. It would appear that at some time following Elizabeth Swift's marriage to John Burden the cottage was either repaired or rebuilt. Although the Broadwater parish registers record a John and Elizabeth Burden, with a son Peter, there is no entry relating to their marriage. The property then descended through the Burden family from Elizabeth to her son Peter in 1703 and after Peter's death in 1758 to his youngest son Thomas Burden, a farmer who had married Ann Gates on 19th July 1750. In August 1791 Thomas Burden senior died and his will bequeathed his copyhold property to his son, Thomas Burden junior, also a farmer, whose wife was Ann (nee Sowter). This marriage only lasted eight years as Ann died at the age of 29 in 1781. In 1796 Thomas married Mary Lamberley, a widow. It was this Thomas Burden who was asked to prepare a map of the town's boundaries after the ancient ceremony of treading the bounds was carried out in 1813. (A copy of an early plan of Worthing, also drawn by Thomas Burden, exists in Worthing Reference Library. It is undated but is believed to have been prepared shortly before the 'Inclosure Act' of 1805, perhaps to assist the Commissioners in implementing the Act.)

From the latter part of the eighteenth century the description of the property was 'a customary messuage or tenement, garden, and one acre more or less'. This old house appears to be the same property that was later known as Alma Cottage (No. 76 High Street) and is illustrated in various books on Worthing.[76] This house was probably named to commemorate the Battle of the Alma during the Crimean War, when on 20th September 1854 the British and their allies defeated the Russians. It was a popular name for smaller houses and cottages during that period and there are several with this name in the villages around the Worthing area. This cottage survived well into the twentieth century but was

Fig. 30 *Alma Cottage*

badly damaged by fire in May 1946 and after having stood derelict, was demolished in April 1948.[77]

A further cottage, marked 23 on Fig. 27, was erected by Thomas Burden in 1762, adjoining the northern end of his own cottage on the north west corner of his garden. This was commemorated by a stone over the porch of the new house which was inscribed 'Thos. & Ann Burden, 1762.' His tenant was Alex. Burden - presumably a relative of Thomas. It was not, however, until 1780 that the manorial court books of Worthing record that the cottage was surrendered by Thomas Burden to the use of Alex Burden, who was then officially admitted as the tenant. Alex died in 1810, aged 77, and John Balcombe, who let out donkey and pony chaises for hire, took over the cottage. This cottage also survived into the twentieth century, but was demolished in 1960 for road improvements.

To the south of Burden's old farmhouses was another ancient freehold property, marked 25 on Fig. 27, which in the mid-seventeenth century was occupied by Thomas Campion when it was described as 'a messuage, barn and garden and 7 acres of land known as Cookes'. When Thomas Campion died in 1647 his will required his executors to sell the property to pay off his debts etc. and any remaining money was to be shared amongst his wife and children. At some time during the second half of the seventeenth century Edward Walker acquired the property, possibly from the sale by Campion's executors. Edward Walker's wife Elizabeth survived him and is recorded as tenant from at least 1673 until her death in 1690, when the property passed to her son Thomas Walker who came from Lindfield.[78] For many years the farm was known as Walker's Farm. After further transactions in 1702 and 1713 the property was acquired by Richard Newland from Richard Barham, the elder, of Lindfield. It was held by the Newland family for many years and in 1827 the house was known as Newland's Farmhouse. For some obscure reason the farmhouse was called the 'Manor House' from c. 1848.[79] This is puzzling since the house was built on Broadwater manor land and has **no** connection whatsoever with the manor of Worthing. The house was a lodging house for many years and eventually in c. 1939 became the offices of Searle's Manor Garage. There are no further references to the house in Worthing directories after 1951 and it was later demolished.

To the south of Newland's old farmhouse was another farmstead of Broadwater manor (marked 26 on Fig 27). This property was owned by John Stempe, husbandman of Worthing, until his death in 1624 when it was inherited by his only daughter Mary Stempe who married John Monke of Worthing. The property was described as 'A messuage or tenement and Barne and 18 acres of land, arable, meadow and pasture lying in the several parishes of Worthing and Heene' and after Mary's death in 1646 it passed to her son Thomas Monke. In 1668 Thomas Monke sold the property to John Sherwood, a blacksmith of West Grinstead, for £216-17s-3d. It was at this time in the occupation of Thomas King. This was not unusual, for the records relating to Worthing show that very few of these early owners actually occupied their property. Up until 1716 the farm was in the possession of John Sherwood and it was referred to as 'Sherwood's Farm' as late as 1792, even though the executors of John Sherwood had sold the property to William Hersee of Lancing in 1723 for £240. In 1735 Nicholas Roberts, a mariner of Brighthelmstone, purchased the property from Charles Hersee of Lancing, the son of William Hersee. By 1752 the property was being farmed by Edward Hoare of Worthing. Elizabeth Brapple, spinster of Brighthelmstone, was named in the will of Nicholas Roberts and by 1762 she held the property. Thirty years later in 1792 she conveyed it to Mr. John Newland for £900. In 1805 John Newland prepared a claim for the impending 'Inclosure Act' concerning his lands belonging to the farm, then known as 'Brapples' (named after the previous owner). The land amounted to a total of 7.5 acres. The house appears to have been let to various tenants until c. 1818 after which no further entries have been found. The house, barn and other buildings were all pulled down in 1822 and consequently the only information known about the house is that contained in John Stempe's probate inventory of 1624.[80] This reveals that the rooms in the early house were described as one lower-chamber, the Hall, milkhouse and kitchen on the ground floor and above these were the '2 Bed Chamber' and the 'Easte lofte'. No further building took place on this site until the first half of the twentieth century.

To the south of Sherwood's farm was a property (marked 27 on Fig 27) described as 'a messuage and garden and orchard in Worthing on the east side of Worthing Street'. In January 1690 it was occupied by Thomas Kinge, a brewer of Worthing, who was the eldest son of William and Mary Kinge. This was possibly the same Thomas Kinge recorded as the occupier of Sherwood's farm two years earlier in 1688. The property was freehold and held of Broadwater manor, and various owners can be traced during the early part of the eighteenth century, most of whom appear to have let their property. In 1702 it was occupied by Daniel Avery and in 1731 by George Lingoe. According to the Land Tax lists Christopher Corfe (yeoman of Worthing) had acquired the property by at least 1780 and was both owner and occupier. After his death his widow continued to occupy the premises and by 1808 James Corfe (eldest son and heir of Christopher), a baker, was recorded in the property. Later Mr. Piggott, also a baker and confectioner, occupied the building. Currently an antique shop, which retains the name of 'Toby Jug' (formerly a restaurant), with bow windows on the top floor still survives on the site. This building is undoubtedly old and is possibly the original house, having been modified and extended during the Georgian period.

Fig. 31 *Burden's cottage (1762)*

Fig. 32 *Manor House (High Street)*

Fig. 33 *'The Toby Jug'*

Part of the garden to the north of this property was subdivided into two small plots of land which were sold and by *c.* 1789 two further houses had been erected fronting Worthing Street. The residue of the garden at the rear of these was, however, retained as part of the original property. Records indicate that William Paine, blacksmith of Broadwater, owned both of them by 1792. Edward Snewin records that the house immediately adjoining 'The Toby Jug' on the north was once occupied by Richard Hide the miller, brother of Mr. Edward Hide who built the smock mill at Navarino. The other house, immediately to the north was the house of Mr. William Tayler, one of the 'Accommodation' coachmen.[81] Both these houses still survive today.

Immediately to the south of 'The Toby Jug' is the modern Charlecote Road, 'Crown House' and two smaller houses. Over 150 years of rebuilding has obliterated the early topography of this area and to assist in the consideration of its early history Fig. 35 is a conjectural map of the area in *c.* 1780 which has been derived from the information contained in the various historical documents. There were two original sites in this area by the eighteenth century and probably long before that. The largest of the two was held from the manor of Broadwater and was described as 'All that messuage, barn and buildings, one orchard of one acre called Gills (Giles) together with 7 acres of land (in the open fields),' when it was sold to John Booker, saddler of Arundel, by Henry Allen of Piddlehinton, Dorset, clerk, in 1711. In September 1751 Elizabeth Booker, widow of John Booker, and her eldest son, also John, sold for £15 the house and garden (marked 28 on Fig 35) separately from the orchard to Edward Hoare, farmer of Worthing. It would appear that Hoare was already occupying the site at the time of the sale and the property was redefined as a 'messuage, garden plot of ground and backside thereto belonging called by the name of Gills (Giles) in Worthing, containing by estimation 18 roods'. By December of the same year (1751) Edward Hoare had sold the property to William Langley of Worthing, husbandman, who died in *c.* 1785. After his death his son John Langley, a farmer of Bognor, sold the house to John Bacon a Worthing fisherman. At his death in 1826 John left the house in his will to his wife Jane and it is this house that Edward Snewin refers to as 'Aunt Jenny's Cottage'.[82] (John's widow was known locally as Jenny.)

Between John Bacon's house and the present High Street was the smaller site, part of Lancing manor (the old manor of St. John's). By 1778 this had been sold by John Newland to John Mitchell who built two houses on the site, one for himself (marked 29 on Fig. 35) and the other for his brother Thomas Mitchell (marked 30 on Fig 35). The remainder of Booker's original land parcel (the orchard) was sold to Charles Bushby of Arundel by 1792. In 1798 his son Thomas Bushby sold the orchard of one acre to Ambrose Cartwright, a carpenter and builder from Worthing, for £126. From 1800 there was a great deal of new building on these two sites, the exact chronology of which is difficult to determine from the limited information available. The relevant part of the 1852 Ordnance Survey map, however, records the properties in great detail and is reproduced as Fig. 36.

By January 1800 Ambrose Cartwright had built a substantial house on his site immediately to the south of the 'Toby Jug', which, in the October of that year, he sold together with the orchard to Richard Penfold of Broadwater, yeoman, for £802-10s-0d. In 1801 Richard Penfold and John Bacon, who lived in Giles old house, wanted to build an access roadway, 16 feet wide (*c.* 5 metres) from Worthing Street (High Street) to their

Fig 34 Houses to the north of the 'Toby Jug'

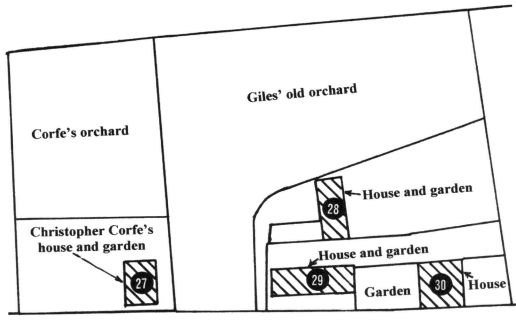

Fig. 35 '*Giles*' *property (c. 1780)*

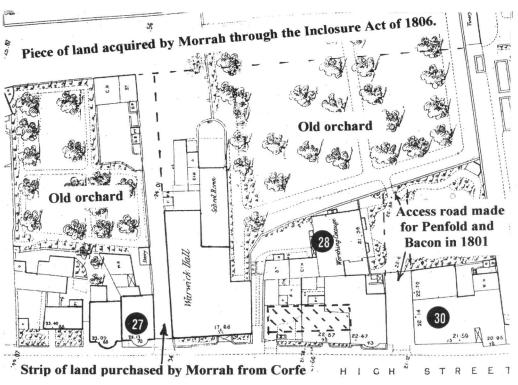

Fig. 36 '*Giles*' *property in 1852*

properties. The Mitchells agreed and it was built. The road is marked on Fig. 36. In June 1801 Michael Morrah of Worthing, a surgeon, purchased the property from Richard Penfold for £1300 and it became both his home and surgery.

Fig. 37 *Michael Morrah's house*

An additional piece of land adjoining his property on the east was acquired by Michael Morrah as part of the re-allocation of land under the Inclosure Act of 1805. In 1809 he also purchased a strip of land from the baker James Corfe, who resided next door (in the later 'Toby Jug') to provide an access to his outbuildings at the rear of his property and his new piece of land. The house was later named Warwick Hall and became a school with the school room built at the rear. The house stood until 1904/5 when it was demolished and by 1905 the Fire Station was built on the site. During the early twentieth century Charlecote Road was also laid out between the Fire Station and the 'Toby Jug'.

John Bacon's old house (marked 28 on Fig 36) was eventually rebuilt to become a boys' school kept by a Mr. Head which later moved to Byron Road. Part of Giles old orchard was acquired and became part of this property which was no doubt the reason for its new name of Orchard House (see Fig. 40). By the 1920's it was recorded as a Girls' Friendly Society and hostel and later re-named Charlecote perhaps during or after the construction of Charlecote Road. In *c.* 1970 it was demolished along with the Fire Station, which had been replaced by a new building constructed for the County Fire Service in 1962 on the south side of Broadwater Green.[83] During the early 1970's the site was redeveloped as the Crown Offices initially to accommodate the Department of Employment, Health and Social Security and Inland Revenue[-the Inspector of Taxes–Worthing 1 Area]. It was completed by the end of 1972, and initially housed in excess of 200 civil servants.[84] This building still exists today.

Fig. 38 *The old Fire Station*

By 1852 John Mitchell's old house was no longer there and its location (marked 29 on Fig 36) is shown dotted. The house was left to Hannah Mitchell (daughter of Thomas Mitchell) in John's will. After her death it was to pass to John's nephews, Richard and James Mitchell. Apparently Hannah became insane and Richard died, leaving the property to James. In 1810 the house and garden was sold to Michael Morrah and by 1821 the house was occupied by Edmund and Hannah Bland. However by 1838 it had been demolished.

Phillip's map of 1814 shows an additional house adjoining to the southern end of Mitchell's old house (marked 29 on Fig. 36) which, according to Edward Snewin was known as 'Challon's High House' and was occupied by Dr. Harris, the partner of Michael Morrah.[85] Although the authors were unable to find anyone with the name 'Challon' connected with this property, there was a Charles Callend occupying the house in 1821. Should it have been Callend's High House? By 1920 the house was re-named High View and the reason for both these names is apparent from the photograph reproduced as Fig. 39. Later the house was converted into flats.

When Mitchell's old house was demolished another small house was built adjoining Challon's High House. Edward Snewin records that it was originally built as a consulting room and surgery for Dr. Harris who married Ellen Morrah the daughter of Michael Morrah.[86] Both these houses are shown as one property in the Hide Survey of 1838 but they eventually became two separate properties. The smaller building became John Knight's dairy by the 1920's. Both houses were occupied until 1960 but were demolished by 1969. Part of the site is now covered by Crown House.

To the south of Challon's High House was the remainder of this area. On this small piece of land prior to 1778 was the house of Thomas Mitchell (marked 30 on Fig. 35). A

Fig. 39 *Challon's High House*

Fig. 40 *Side view of Orchard House*

butcher's shop was erected on the site by 1794 and by 1810 James Mitchell had sold the house, shop and garden to John Pullen, Worthing's first butcher, who was probably the earlier occupant of the site. Pullen is still recorded as occupier by 1828. A house still stands on this site and this may well be the original house. During the twentieth century it was occupied by a furniture dealer and Harold Wilson the antiques dealer. Adjoining the house

Fig. 41 'Giles' site from roof of Ann Street car park

to the south was another house erected by 1819 which was occupied by Edward Purser for at least twenty years. This building also still stands today and from *c.* 1937 was also occupied by Harold Wilson the antiques dealer for many years.

There were several houses in the hamlet that were occupied by inhabitants who were involved in fishing. However, only one house location has been positively identified, from the three Worthing probate inventories specifying fishermen, and that is the house of David Symonds in 1671. It was located just to the north of the old Rivoli site and is marked 11 on Fig 19. The house had two rooms at ground level, a kitchen and a 'low chamber' with a loft over one of the rooms. The house is recorded in the 1664 and 1665 Hearth Tax lists as having one hearth, which correlates with the probate inventory where all the fire tools were recorded in the kitchen.[87] After Symonds' death his will, dated 22nd April 1671, devised the property to his wife Alice to sell to pay his debts. Alice married John Stempe of Sompting, a shepherd, and in 1692 they sold the house to William Wade, rector of Broadwater. The house was recorded in 1738 but does not appear later on Yeakell and Gardner's map of *c.* 1780, and it can only be assumed that it had been demolished. The sites of the houses of the other two fishermen, John Campion in 1632 [88] and John Martin in 1628 [89] have, as yet, to be identified.

Although John Stoneham's probate inventory of 1682 does not specify his occupation the amount of fishing equipment recorded indicates that he was involved in fishing activities.[90] His house, marked 32 on Fig. 19, was sited on a one-acre piece of land held of Lancing manor (the old manor of St. John's) at the junction of the modern Brighton Road and High Street. Prior to this in 1645 the cottage had belonged to Michael Wheateley, when Thomas Harman of Findon, 'a poor, lame, impotent person', with his wife and two children (who were previously charged to the parish of Findon) came to stay. However, complaints by the parishioners of Broadwater curtailed their visit, for at the Quarter Sessions it was ordered that Thomas Harman and his family be 'forthwith sent back to Findon'. After John Stoneham's death in 1682 the property passed to Mary, his only daughter and heir, who was the wife of John Soper. The property was subsequently purchased by John Booker of Arundel and descended through his family until it was sold in December 1778 to John Luther (who built Warwick House - see Chapter 4), when the annual rent was one penny. The property was described in the Lancing manorial court books as 'a tenement and barn which some years ago fell down or was pulled down and a piece of land containing one acre (formerly Wheatleys, since Stonehams, since John Soper's)'. Once the buildings were demolished the land was described as 'Soper's plat'. It finally disappeared under the front lawn of Warwick House. There were other fishermen recorded at various houses in the hamlet during the latter part of the eighteenth century. Two of these were the houses of William Badger, marked 33 on Fig 19, and John Hickox, marked 8 on Fig. 19.

Since the Sussex coastal plain borders the sea it is not surprising to find numerous references to fishermen and sailors in the various records. It is known that over the centuries the coastline has undergone changes due to the continual encroachment of the sea onto the land, abnormal storms and changes in sea level. Often this also resulted in whole or parts of villages being washed away. Nevertheless the sea also provided food and a livelihood (both legal and illegal). Evidence of fishing can be found in the Domesday text, shipbuilding is recorded from the medieval period, while smuggling and wrecking were renowned along the coast.

There is evidence to show that fishing has been practised by the inhabitants of the Sussex coastal settlements for centuries. It has been suggested that in the seventh century AD St. Wilfred taught the fishermen of Selsey how to catch fish from the open sea with nets, since all they could do previously was to take 'the eels which they found in the muddy inlets and estuaries at low tide'.[91]

Fig. 42 *The house of John Hickox*

Records show that in the latter half of the twelfth century, the Bishop of Chichester's fishermen at Hove had a net at Yarmouth - and also a net for mackerel fishing and in 1341 the value of the tithe of fish from Hove was 20 shillings.[92] In 1385 there was a thriving fishing industry at Lancing, and Worthing was described as a small agricultural and fishing hamlet in the medieval period.[93]

During the seventeenth century it is apparent from surviving Vice Admiralty court papers for Sussex (1638–1668) that visitations were held annually when citations were issued in the Lord High Admiral's name for all seamen and fishermen to appear before the commissary. These citations went to the constables of all those Hundreds adjacent to the coast who were required to cause the tithing man to make a return of the seamen and fishermen and to warn them to appear at the Town Hall of Chichester or Brighton and, on one occasion, Arundel Sessions house, the fine for non-attendance being 6s-8d. Despite this it appears from the returns that not all the seamen attended, perhaps only one attending for each boat, just sufficient to form a Hundred Jury which dealt with all manner of Admiralty offences.[94] The average number of seamen shown in the returns by each tithing man reveal that the largest returns were for the parishes of Lancing with 15 seamen, Selsey with 14 and Bracklesham with 10. The return for Broadwater was 5.

The probate inventories for Broadwater and Worthing only positively identify three fishermen while one or two others, although not specifying the deceased's occupation, record equipment that shows an involvement with fishing. Detailed information concerning the lifestyle of the seventeenth-century fishermen at Worthing is, therefore, very sparse and because of this further relevant information was obtained from the 38 surviving probate inventories for the coastal plain parishes in Sussex during the period 1610–1719 which specify fisherman as the deceased's occupation. Nine further inventories were found showing the deceased's occupation as either mariner or seamen. It is probable that these seamen were deep-sea fishermen, although this is not conclusive.

From an analysis of the inventories it is evident that the fishermen occupied the lower half of the social hierarchy, their average T.E.V. indicating Group 3 (Lower Middling). Fishing was, of necessity, a seasonal occupation and a detailed analysis of their inventories revealed that most of them were unable to exist by fishing alone and probably spent part of the year as farmers or labourers. David Symonds of Worthing is recorded as a fishermen in his probate inventory[95] but is described elsewhere as a labourer. Overall fishing equipment represented 22% of the fisherman's total goods and chattels while farming equipment, tools and animals accounted for a further 16%. It was also evident that many of the yeomen and husbandmen of the coastal plain parishes also supplemented their livelihood by fishing, together with others who did not have a full-time trade or occupation.[96] This was also clearly evident from a detailed examination of all the probate inventories for the parish of Broadwater.

When recording and valuing the fishermen's tools and equipment the assessor(s) often used terminology which today has become obsolete or perhaps unfamiliar. Fortunately the fishermen who operated from Brighton, on the extreme eastern fringe of the Sussex coastal plain, left a record of their fishing activities during Tudor times. As a consequence of sending a petition to the Privy Council in 1579 (concerning their local problems) the fishermen were ordered to meet and

'sette down in wrytinge their ancient customs and orders concerning the true makinge payment and imployinge of the contribution known as the Quarter share'.

This they did in 1580 and it is from this record that much of the information concerning the early fishing industry and related terminology has been extracted.[97]

The records identify eight separate 'fares' or fisheries. The local or inshore fisheries were 'Tucknet' for plaice, 'Drawnet' for mackerel, 'Harbour' for conger and 'Cock' for herring, all engaging boats of up to eight tons. Those employed further afield for deep sea fishing were 'Shotnet' for mackerel, 'Scarborough' for cod, 'Yarmouth' and 'Flew' both for herring, all with boats exceeding eight tons. Apart from the fisheries at Scarborough and Yarmouth it appears that the Brighton boats also sailed eastwards to the North Foreland and beyond to catch herring from the shoals moving from the North Sea to the north French coast, and mackerel from the shoals moving southwards down the Suffolk coast into the Channel.[98]

The method employed by the Brighton fishermen was to divide the profits of the catch into shares. There were shares for the men, the boat and nets, the vicar, the master and the usual quarter share for the churchwardens. The number and division of the shares basically depended on the size of the boat, the number of men employed and the amount of nets and lines they could take. Fishermen from other parishes were accepted into the Brighton boats under the same conditions. No such documentary evidence has been found for the remainder of the coastal plain and it is, in the main, the seventeenth- and early eighteenth-century probate returns and wills that provide any further information on the fishermen of West Sussex.

Although probate inventories record numerous items of fishing equipment, they are not very informative regarding boats as most were given general descriptions like 'great', 'small' or 'old' etc. and only four types were actually recorded., namely 'barke' (barque), 'hoi' (hoy), 'flewcock' and 'pink'. The following extracts from local inventories are typical examples. The inventory of Robert Hoell, thatcher of Worthing, in 1675 records 'of seagoods, one olde boat and 10 netts prized at £3-10s-8d.', while that of Robert Johnson of Broadwater in 1681, 'for pt. (part) of a vessell at sea -£30-0s-0d' and for John Campyon, fisherman of Worthing in 1631/2 'flewcock with the Tacklinge belonging unto hir', which he left in his will to his son Thomas.[99] Although the total number of boats recorded in the West Sussex probate inventories for fishermen is 33, suggesting an average of almost one per inventory, several inventories contained more than one, thus leaving five deceased fishermen with no boat at all. It is most likely that these sailed with others who owned boats. The common practice throughout Northern Europe at this time was for ownership of a boat to be divided into equal parts or shares which were divisors of four, the smallest being a 64th. This method assisted in raising capital and spreading the risk since there was no insurance available at that time.[100] Although this method was adopted at Brighton and there are comparable instances of recorded ownership of one quarter, one eighth and one sixteenth parts of a boat in the inventories of other coastal plain parishes, an example being 'a sixteenth of a pink - £12-10s-0d' in that of Mary Howell (widow of Worthing, 1709)[101] it seems to have been less strictly adhered to outside Brighton, for the inventory of John Martin, fisherman of Worthing, dated 1628 records not only 'a quarter of a boat with that belonging to her - 10s-0d.' but also, a third of a boat with that belonging to her - 16s-0d.'

In 1653 it was written that 'there are a few good things in Sussex: a Selsey cockle, a Chichester lobster, Arundel mullet and an Amberley trout.'[102] There is no doubt that crabs and lobsters were caught, since there are in excess of 200 pots of all types recorded in the inventories, described variously as out-pots, small pots, lobster pots and crab–pots. These pots or 'creels' were baited with fresh or decaying fish. It also appears that trout, mullet, dabs, sole and plaice were mainly caught by the use of drag-nets or draw-nets of which several are recorded in the inventories.

Any indications of deep sea fishing by the coastal plain fisherman can only be surmised from the nets recorded in the inventories. Over half the nets were for herring, some 78 out of the overall total of 154, which included 'two old Hering netts' valued at 10s–0d in the Worthing Inventory of Henry Stoneham.[103] The 'nine "flew" nets" valued at 30s-0d in the inventory of John Campyon dated 1631/2 indicate that some of the Worthing fishermen, like their neighbours at Brighton, also exploited the North Sea fishing grounds.

Other miscellaneous items found in the inventories of those described as fishermen include buoys, anchors, hallyers and poles. In some instances a general description of 'sea craft', 'sea venture', 'sea-faringthings' and even 'sea-goods' was used to cover a miscellany of fishing items.

During the seventeenth century the majority of the fishermen in Brighton lived in 'Lower' Brighton which was situated on the beach below the low cliffs. A rental of Brighthelmstone in 1665 records that this lower town contained streets, the Castle Inn, fishermen's houses and cottages, shops, stake places, capstans and parcels of land rented for buildings or any of the foregoing uses. An analysis of the rental shows a total of 18 cottages/houses, 63 shops, 18 capstans, 23 stake-places and 45 parcels of land.[104] The shops were workshops in which the fishermen stored their nets and tackle, repaired items and prepared their locally caught fish. The stake places were the places their boats were kept when pulled ashore by capstans. A somewhat similar situation existed at Hove, to the west of Brighton, where the small cliff still existed but tapered away to the west. In the court rolls for Hove, cottages, shops and land were again described as 'under the cliffe' as at Brighton.

The use of Shops by fisherman in West Sussex is confirmed by the inventory of Richard Bridger of Siddlesham dated 1630 in which, under the heading of 'In the Shopp' are listed '23 yarmouth, flew netts, 4 ropes to the yarmouth nett etc.'[105] During the seventeenth century shops are recorded at both Lancing and Worthing when, in c. 1620, King James I 'made fishing grants of the beach at Lancing and Broadwater'.[106] At Lancing a map dated 1622 shows 'Lancinge Shopps' on the beach together with boats opposite 'the Damme'[107] which today survives as Shopsdam Road. This site formerly contained a sixteenth-century landing stage where various boats were loaded and unloaded in 1566[108] and this is shown as 'Launcinge Stade' on a map of 1587 prepared for the defence of the Sussex coast against the Spanish Armada[109] (see Fig. 44). The word 'stade' is derived from the Anglo-Saxon language and is defined variously as a bank, a shore where ships can be beached or a landing place, similar to the 'Staithes' at Hastings.[110] It appears likely that the seventeenth-century 'stake-place' emanated from the same source.

The Armada map also shows a lagoon named 'Penhowse', thought to have been the site of the old port of Pende (thirteenth to fifteenth century) which by 1587 was no longer useable due to the silting of the channel leading to it. The provision of a landing stage, sited nearly opposite 'Penhowse' probably resulted from the loss of the old port. In 1608 the site of the earlier landing stage was described as 'a parcell of waste or common called 'Launceing Have' (Haven), undoubtedly a reference to the old port of Pende.[111] By 1609 the King had seized the site for the crown, since this was normal practice for derelict or waste land, and appended it to his own manor of St. John which had widely scattered small pieces of land and property in New Shoreham, Lancing and Worthing. This manor was later in private hands and shops were recorded on the site until 1803.[112] The site is now covered by the sea.

Since the right to the foreshore was vested in the lords of the coastal manors in Sussex, a shop could only be erected with the permission of the lord upon payment of an annual rent. According to the court rolls at Hove, the average size of a parcel of land for a shop building was a rectangle whose length and width were no smaller than 50 feet [15 metres] and no greater than 60 feet [18 metres].[113] The shops were built of wood with a tarred roof and were usually fastened to the ground. An analysis of the court rolls for Hove and Brighton shows the annual rent of a shop or cottage on the beach ranged between 2d in 1576 and 4d in 1665, while the most common rent for a parcel of land, capstan, or a stake-place was 6d.

At Worthing 'a shop with other sea-crafte' valued at £8[115] is recorded as early as 1612 in the inventory of John Kempe, yeoman. The inventory of John Stoneham, also from

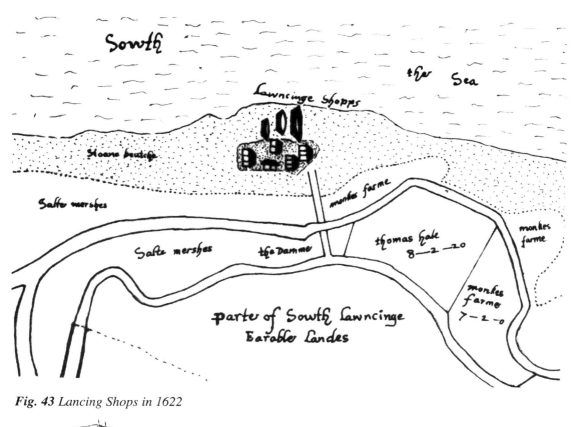

Fig. 43 *Lancing Shops in 1622*

Fig. 44 *The 'Armada' map*

Fig. 45 *Budgen's map of 1724 showing Worthing Shops*

Worthing, records amongst other fishing items, 'an old boat and capstone' (Capstan) and also 'part of an old shop'. It was, however, the inventory of John Campion of Worthing, fisherman, dated 1632 that locates the site of these shops at Worthing, for it records 'one shoppe upon the stoane beatch'. Like boats, the shops were often in part ownership, generally shared by two people as can be seen in the Brighton rental where 'halfe a shoppe near the Portallgate the other half being Thomas Paynes, late Derrick Paynes –2d.'[116] At Worthing the inventory of John Martin dated 1628 records 'Halfe a shoppe at 12s-0d'.[117]

During the seventeenth century the south coast fishing industry steadily declined. This was partly due to the ravages of war. From 1597 the continuing war with Spain appears to have left the south coast in an unsettled state, greatly affecting the fishermen, their ships having been continually attacked by the Spaniards and the 'Dunkirks'.[118] Later the Thirty Years War with the French, the English Civil War and three Dutch wars all caused great distress to the south coast fisheries. Between 1609 and 1666 there were at least three petitions to Parliament from the 'poor and distressed fishermen of Brighthelmstone' complaining that they were impeded by the enemy from fishing voyages, of attacks on their shipping, the loss of boats laden with merchandise, and the capture and loss of life. In the 1620's fishing at Shoreham was also said to be decayed and impeded by enemy action and during the 1670's only three fishermen were listed there,[119] while in *c.* 1642 a petition from the 'poor fishermen at Lancing' outlined their problems concerning loss of trade and poverty.[120]

Coastal erosion was also a major factor in the gradual decline of the fishing industry. At Brighton the landward movement of an off-shore bar known to be fronting the coast on either side of the Adur estuary in *c.* 1680, was probably affecting the lower fishing town by *c.* 1640. By 1665 twenty-two tenements under the cliff had been lost to the sea and the

fishermen were pushed further up the beach.[121] During the next forty years, more and more
tenements, capstans and shops were washed away by the relentless movement of the sea,
culminating in two terrible storms in 1703 and 1705 when a total of 113 fishermen's shops,
cottages, capstans and stake places were completely destroyed and buried under a mound of
beach. The sea was now lapping the base of the cliffs.[122] The fishing community at
Brighton was devastated by these two major storms.

At Worthing the shingle bar had formed offshore by the late sixteenth century.
During the seventeenth century, as a result of silting, a large area of land, known later as the
'salt green', 'salt-grass' or Worthing Common, gradually came into being between the bar
and the modern shore-line.[114] In distinct contrast to Brighton this area was used as a
common pasture on which inhabitants of the hamlet of Worthing had certain common rights
for their animals. Entries in the Broadwater court books for the early part of the eighteenth
century record they had 'Leazes' (leases) to graze their animals. A single lease entitled
them to put one bullock on the common. If they had two leases they were allowed one horse
and a sheep lease allowed them one sheep for every acre they held. If these limits were
exceeded they were penalised by fines set between sixpence and twenty shillings depending
on the animals involved. A typical example of an infringement is recorded in the court
books for 1709

> 'Wee present Thomas Parsons for bringing into the comons of the manor ffoure
> hundred sheep for his 22 acres and a halfe of land contrary to the Order and
> Agreement of the Lord and Tenants of this manor made at the court held on 1st
> October 1700'

Although not specifically recorded in any of the documents researched it is inconceivable
that the flat area of Worthing Common, with virtually no defence against the sea, was not
also ravaged by these storms. The cumulative effects of the continual encroachment of the
sea onto the Worthing Common is, however, shown on the 1748 map of Worthing on the

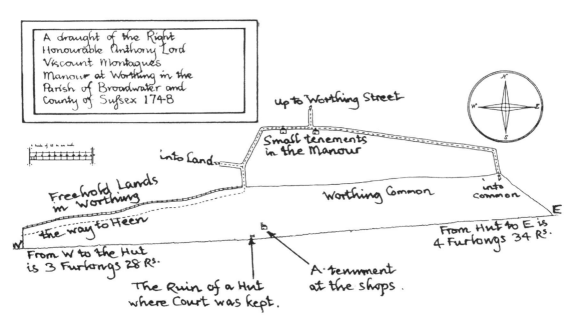

Fig. 46 *A reduced copy of the 1748 map of Worthing on which the notes have been written
in a similar style of handwriting and spelling to that of the original*

previous page.

Although the privilege of the ancient 'right of wreck' (see Chapter 2) still prevailed during the eighteenth and nineteenth centuries no entries have been found in the Worthing or Broadwater Court Rolls prior to the eighteenth century. This possibly explains the widespread practice on the coast of Sussex of illicit plundering (known as 'wrecking'). In a letter dated November 1629 Sir W. Covert records that a Dunkirk Ship was driven ashore at Worthing by the states men-of-war. Although the crew of 66 were saved the 'country people according to their inhuman custom had seized the goods and spoilt the ship'.[123]

In the early part of the eighteenth century the right of the foreshore at Worthing was clearly held by Broadwater manor. The manorial court books record the lord of the manor's claim's to the ancient 'right of wreck' on his foreshore. In 1709 the Reeve of Lancing manor seized a mast of a ship considered to be on the Broadwater side of the boundary and as a consequence the boundaries of the manor were re-emphasised and the following was recorded in the court book,

> 'wee present that the Bounds and Lymitts of this Mannor Reach and Extend on the
> Sea-shore from Heene Comon to South Launcinge'.

At a Court Baron held on 15th July 1711 it was recorded that a piece of timber was taken up as a 'wreck of the sea-shore' and further entries in 1718 and 1728 record 'a raft of ship timber' and 'a mast and several planks' taken from Worthing Common. It is of interest to note that the only recorded instance of a 'Sea-Reeve' actually being appointed at Broadwater to check the beach for items washed ashore and claim them for the lord of the Manor was in 1713. Broadwater manor's assertion to the 'right of wreck' appears to have been unchallenged until an entry was made in the court book of Worthing manor on the 25th August 1747. Under the heading 'customs presented' it is recorded,

> '.....the Lord of the Manor is entitled to all wrecks at sea which come on shore on
> the said Manor. And that the Lord's Manor extends from Worthing Shops to certain
> Rayles about 4 furlongs distante to the west and from the said shops to a certaine
> Lane called the East Lane to the east.'

This entry led to a dispute between the lords of the manor of Broadwater and Worthing and the map of 1748 depicting 'the Rt. Hon. Anthony Lord Viscount Montagues Manour at Worthing' was undoubtedly produced to support the claim made in his Court Rolls. The dispute went to arbitrators who decided that Worthing beach, extending from Heene to Lancing, was parcel of the manor of Broadwater and that John Butler as lord of that Manor was entitled to all 'wreck thrown on Shoar at the said Beache'. No further entries relating to this matter were found in the Worthing Court books, but Broadwater manor continued claiming 'wrecks of the sea' between 1767 and 1819.

Part of the 1748 map has been redrawn with additional features and notes annotated on it derived from the authors' research and this is reproduced as Fig. 47. The map shows 'A tenument at the shops' (marked 40 on Fig. 47), the shops being those of the fishermen built on the beach but unfortunately not shown on the original map. In 1705 a grant was made to Thomas Maddox of a messuage or cottage 'lately erected on the beach at Worthing' at a rent of 6d per annum. This house still survived in 1726 when it was recorded 'we present the shop adjoining to Maddox house upon the sea beach to be in the manor of Broadwater'. In July 1748 it was recorded that Richard Fitzhenry and William Humphreys had 'lately erected 2 cottages upon the Beach being part of the waste of the manor without the leave or License of the Lord of the manor'. As any structure erected on the beach would be prone to continual movement, it is logical to suggest that Thomas Maddox's cottage would have been built of timber, as were the fishermen's huts. This being the case it is highly unlikely that this cottage survived from 1726 to 1748 in such an environment and

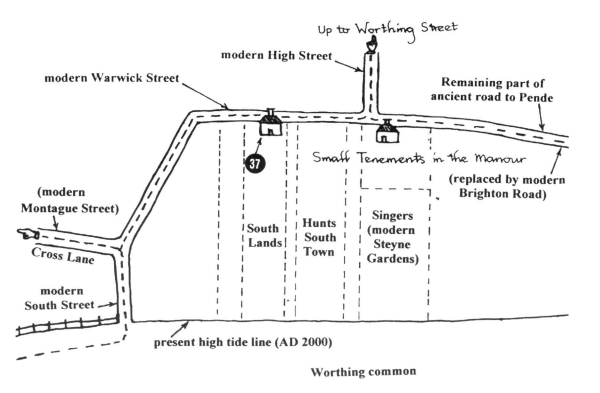

Fig. 47 Enlarged extract of 1748 map with additional notes and features

the tenement shown probably represents one of the two cottages built in 1748. In 1750 David Stone of Thakeham was granted a messuage which was described as the 'Western most house now erected on Worthing Beach'.

By 1762 Thomas Wicks, a victualler of Worthing, had acquired the cottage of William Humphrey for a yearly quit rent of one shilling and had named it the Sea House. At some stage it became the Sea House Inn, presumably serving the needs of the local fishermen rather than visitors, as there are indications of a 'revival' in the fishing industry at Worthing between 1763 and 1773. Worthing supplied fish to Dorking in 1763 and a 'great fishery' was recorded at Worthing in 1773.[124] The sea was, however, still encroaching further onto the common and the position of the Sea House Inn became precarious. Its final demise is recorded in the *Sussex Weekly Advertiser* of 14th December 1772:

> 'About a fortnight ago a little public house on Worthing common in the parish of
> Broadwater, belonging to Thomas Wicks was washed down and buried in the beach,
> which has greatly distressed the unfortunate owner, being a poor man with a large
> family, and whose bread depended on the custom of the house.'

The location of this old house has been described as being opposite Bedford Row on the
sands at low tide about halfway down the length of the present pier. This corresponds
almost exactly with the house marked 40 on Fig. 47. According to Edward Snewin, old
Thomas Lindup the ferryman once showed a young Henry Blann wooden stumps still
protruding from the sands and explained that they were the remains of the old Sea House in
which his wife Mary Summer of Coombes had worked as a servant before their marriage.
Thomas Lindup married her on the 5th August 1777.[126] It was not until 1783 that a new Sea
House Inn was finally built at the bottom of South Street on part of a small open field called
'The Roods' held of Broadwater manor.

The other building shown on the beach, marked 41 on Fig. 47, was 'The Ruin of a
Hut where Court was kept'. This was obviously used by Worthing manor but no record of
its origin can be found in any of the court books. It may well be that prior to its destruction
by the sea, the Sea House Inn on the beach was used for the meetings of Worthing manor's
manorial courts as Public Houses were often used for such gatherings. In 1792 the Steward
of Worthing manor proposed to hold court in the new Sea House Inn. He was, however,
informed that the house was built on Broadwater manor land and was refused permission.

The encroachment of the sea continued and the approaching shingle bar formed a
backwater on the beach which was removed at great expense after complaints by visitors.
By the early part of the nineteenth century the whole of the common had disappeared giving
rise to the fine sandy beach noted during the late eighteenth century.[127]

The fishermen at Worthing continued to build their huts on the beach for the storage
of nets, oars, sails etc. but as the number of houses increased in the early years of the
nineteenth century, shops for the sale of fish, fruit and vegetables were set up on the beach,
fastened into the shingle or clay. At a Court Baron for Broadwater manor in October 1810
it was recorded that for some years past, John Davise, a fishmonger, had paid the lord of the
manor an annual rent of 5 shillings for each of his two fish shops erected on Worthing
Beach. Henry Cooke paid the same rent for his single fish shop. The 'Fish House' shown on
Fig.48 may well be one of those kept by John Davise.

Since the shingle beach had now reached the mainland, many of the inhabitants of the
houses and hotels being erected by the sea beach considered that these huts and shops were
an interruption to the view from their lower windows and complained to the Lord of the
Manor. As a consequence of this, some of the fish houses were placed on wheels in order
that they could be moved from one spot to another, apparently in an attempt to minimise the
problem.

There were two other buildings shown on the 1748 map, the westernmost one of
which (marked 37 on Figs. 19 and 47) can be traced back to the sixteenth century. As no
records have been found for this property in any of the court books examined to date, all the
know information is contained in an 'Abstract of title' for James Heather prepared in 1838
in support of a piece of land, formerly part of this property, when it was sold for
development at the beginning of the nineteenth century. One of the earliest references to
this property is in 1597 when John Hunn of Worthing, yeoman, purchased for £40.0s.0d. 'a
messuage, barn and land' from Nicholas Page of Ringmer, also a yeoman. The house was
built on a 2.75-acre piece of land to the south of modern Warwick Street. With it was also
one rood of land (0.25 acres) in 'Gurrs Corner', part of the West Field (the earliest known
open or common field at Worthing). The house must have been substantial as it was later
described as 'a mansion dwelling-house'. Because of the lack of manorial information on

Fig. 48 *Worthing Fish House (John Nixon, 1805)*

this property it may well be that the house existed as part of the Easebourne Priory 'estate' which was seized by King Henry VIII at the Dissolution of the monasteries in 1536 when it was then possibly sold off independently to the remainder of the land which became the manor of Worthing in 1544. This could well be the reason why no manor house for Worthing manor has been found. When initially constructed the combined revenue from the *c.* 100 acres of the Easebourne Priory 'estate' would have been more than adequate to maintain such a house and its occupants.

In 1662 the property, known as 'South House and Lands', was occupied by Richard Hunn, grandson of John, and at his death his probate inventory shows that he farmed other lands beside his own. He was also a fisherman and the inventory records 'Pte (part) of a boate and nets' valued at £2.10s.0d.[128] Richard was described as a husbandman and his will directed that his house and lands were to be sold to pay his debts and funeral expenses. Any money left over was to be disposed of amongst his children as directed in his will. Accordingly his executors sold the property in 1665 to Edward Howell of Sompting, yeoman, for £60. Thereafter the property descended through the Howell family to Henry Howell whose will in 1786 devised it to his sister Mary Morris, widow, who lived with him. By that date the property was described as 'all that messuage in Worthing with barn, stable, coach house, wash house, garden and all other premises belonging. And all those lands whether arable, meadow or pasture lying in Worthing containing together 10 acres.' In *c.* 1788 Mary Morris married Methuselah Jones of Worthing, gentleman, but this became void when it was found that Jones' first wife was still alive at the time of the marriage.

Later she married William Wicks of Worthing, brickmaker. By *c*. 1790 the old house was demolished and the land divided up and sold off for development.

Open field agriculture continued at Worthing until 1806 when the 'Inclosure Act' was implemented. Although the population of England had virtually doubled during the eighteenth century it was still able to feed itself from its own food production. The standard of living was at last gradually beginning to improve and by 1760 'wheaten bread' was being eaten by nearly half the population. It was no longer just a luxury of the wealthy.[129] Despite limited agricultural experiments and the introduction of some new crops, the daily routine for Worthing's farmers remained relatively unchanged.

The manorial court books, however, provide evidence of an underlying process which ultimately contributed greatly to the demise of the hamlet. The original land holdings within a manor would have consisted of a dwelling house and land ranging from 4 to 14 acres. Many of the early tenants' names were recorded and often retained in the court books to describe these ancient holdings which descended through the centuries. (eg. Lambolds, Dukes, Dawtreys etc.). The records show that from at least the sixteenth century many of these holdings were gradually being tenanted by the more affluent members of society who were amalgamating them into larger, composite estates. The process began as a direct result of the shortage of labour caused by the Black Death in the medieval period and continued for the next two centuries before gathering momentum during the seventeenth and eighteenth centuries. In the eighteenth century outsiders such as John Booker and Charles Bushby from Arundel and James Lloyd of Lancing all held estates. Although individual properties were still controlled by their respective manor, they were viewed by the land holders as part of their larger overall composite estate. A few of the local members of the influential families, such as the Newlands, Lindups and Wicks, were also very quick to seize their opportunities and so by the end of the eighteenth century a few wealthy estate holders controlled the greater part of the land, not only in Worthing, but also in the parish of Broadwater.

4. THE GEORGIAN TOWN

The impetus for the transformation of Worthing from hamlet to town was the fashion for holidays beside the sea, which became part of British culture. The institution of 'going to the seaside' appears to have originated in the north of England during the late seventeenth and early eighteenth century. Doctors had recommended seawater drinking and bathing prior to 1700[1] and by the end of the seventeenth century it was traditional for artisans and country folk in Lancashire to both drink and bathe in seawater at the August spring tide, as it was thought to have 'special powers of purification and regeneration' in addition to being a cure for all manner of diseases.[2] At the beginning of the eighteenth century the therapeutic use of sea bathing was also being practised in South Lancashire, for Nicholas Blundell of Crosby records in his diary that he had arranged for his daughters to be dipped in the sea to cure a skin eruption. His efforts were, however, to no avail for he had to ultimately resort to 'wise women' and a variety of other popular remedies.[3]

Initially there was little interest from the 'leisured wealthy', for they preferred to continue to partake of their therapeutic waters at the spa resorts as an established part of their annual routine. Most remained attracted by the integration of the fashion for drinking and bathing in the spa waters and the organised leisure activities available at the various libraries and assembly rooms supervised by a master of ceremonies.[4] In its early days the popularity of sea bathing grew slowly, but, as the prestige of the medical profession increased, advice from such sources may well have begun to influence a significant minority of the 'leisured classes', for by 1730 Scarborough, Margate and Brighton were all developing a recognisable sea bathing season. The habit of going to the seaside had begun, but was in some respects only an adjunct to the spa season, and it took several generations for the seaside to fully supersede the spa in the affections of many of the affluent seekers after health, pleasure and status in attractive surroundings.[5]

The publication in 1750 of Dr. Richard Russell's book *A Dissertation concerning the use of Sea Water in Diseases of the Glands* provided further momentum to the fashion for seawater cures, as its appearance coincided with an upsurge of interest in such matters and the medical profession soon adopted seawater as the new cure for a variety of disorders that had previously defied their primitive treatments. Dr Russell's move to the fishing village of Brighthelmstone (Brighton) in 1754, to supervise the practical application of his remedies, coincided with an increasing patronage of that village by royalty, and the fashion for these new seawater remedies soon began to affect adjacent areas of the Sussex coastline.

It would appear that Worthing, with its and mild and equable climate, sheltered by the Downs from the north east winds and with more sunshine than elsewhere, especially in winter,[6] was favourably sited to benefit from the limited but growing attraction of sea-bathing and its gently sloping sandy beach[7] was soon discovered. The initial impact on the normal life of those who lived and worked in the hamlet of Worthing was, however, minimal as the early years of the sea bathing fashion offered little, if any, inducement for large scale investment. Visitors only frequented hamlets like Worthing for therapeutic reasons, and the first recorded visitor was a Londoner, who came in 1759 to enjoy the sea air and bathing.[8]

The first 'speculator' to perceive the potential of Worthing as a seaside resort was John Luther who, in 1781, constructed a substantial 'Marine Villa'[9] (marked 42 on Fig. 49) at the south eastern end of Worthing Street on land he had purchased from the

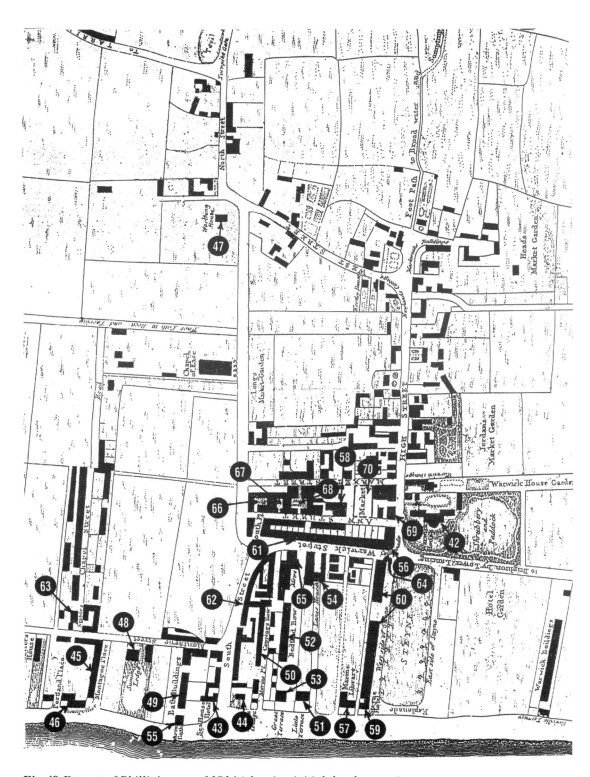

Fig.49 *Extract of Phillip's map of 1814 (showing initial development)*

Fig. 50 *View of Warwick House*

trustees of John Booker of Arundel.[10] Later known as Warwick House, it was built in the prevailing style of the period with flint walls and yellow brick quoins and window reveals, the bricks having been made locally from the blue clay that was to be found on the Worthing Common or Saltgrass. The ground plan was 'T' shaped. The central block had, on the ground floor, a magnificent dining room which measured 20 x 30 feet (approx. 6 x 9 metres), with a deep bow window facing south, a morning room, smoking room, hall and other apartments. On the first floor was a drawing room of similar proportions to the dining room, six principal bedrooms, a boudoir and three servants' bedrooms served by a separate staircase. Above was an attic floor with two further bedrooms, one of which had a balcony. The west wing contained the domestic quarters, while the east wing connected with the stables. The main entrance was on the west side and was approached by a circular drive from Worthing Street, and a second entrance on the north side led to the stables and servants' quarters. Surprisingly, the accommodation did not include a single bathroom.[11]

Very few Georgian resorts were created on virgin sites in the middle of nowhere. Most grew up within or alongside established villages or small towns. Indeed, Worthing was the only rural settlement in Sussex that became a successful early resort town. As a 'gamester', John Luther would undoubtedly have been fully aware of the established annual routine of those who visited the inland spa towns such as Bath and Tunbridge Wells and the new preference of many to partake in sea bathing, apparently as a reaction against the formality and expense of the spas and the increasing cynicism about the claims made by doctors.[12] It may be that his speculative intuition to build a marine residence which could be used by the visiting gentry provided the catalyst for the major transition which took place between 1780 and 1811 when, after years of little perceptible change, the former agricultural and fishing hamlet of Worthing was transformed into a fashionable watering place.

John Luther was a well known Georgian gamester: the Rev. John Evans, in *A Picture of Worthing*,[13] relates very disapprovingly how, on one occasion, Luther was said to have lost £100,000 at the throw of the dice, but only £50,000 was paid. Perhaps this is the reason why only seven years after building this property his trustees were empowered to sell it to the Earl of Warwick from which its later name of Warwick House was derived.

Initially all that was needed for an emerging watering place like Worthing to cater for the small number of initial visitors of moderate means and quieter tastes, that had not been drawn to the more developed resorts such as Brighton and Margate, was an Inn and a few bathing machines. By c. 1783 a successor to the original Sea House, which had been washed away in 1772 as a result of the Sea Common being eroded by the sea, had been opened by a Mr. Hodgkinson under the patronage of Mr. Hogflesh. As the John Nixon watercolour, reproduced below, shows, this new Sea House Inn (marked 43 on Fig.49) was

Fig. 51 John Nixon water colour of the Sea House Inn from the south-west c. 1785

again located close to the beach, on the south-west corner of the seaward end of Worthing Street (today the southern end of modern South Street). Thomas Hogflesh appears to have purchased the property by 1786,[14] and in 1789 Rice and Co., builders from Brighton, seeing the potential for investment as the number of visitors to the hamlet continued to increase, added a larger two-storey extension together with stables and coach houses to the rear.[15]

It would appear that Rice and Co. were not alone in seeing the potential for investment in Worthing's initial transformation into a fashionable watering place for, in the same year as they extended the Sea House Inn, Grove and Co. opened the New Inn, which was similar in size and appearance, under the patronage of James Austin.[16] As the further watercolour by John Nixon (reproduced as Fig. 52) reveals, the New Inn (marked 44 on Fig. 49) was located on the south-east corner of Worthing Street, immediately opposite the Sea House Inn. By 1792 it had been purchased by Killick and Co. and the new patron was Richard Bacon. The Sea House Inn and New Inn, 'both close to the beach, from the windows of which (were) pleasing views of the ocean',[17] were essential resort amenities,

Fig. 52 *New Inn and Sea House Inn (Nixon)*

for they not only provided accommodation for visitors who sought lodgings, but also offered food, horses and carriages, and very quickly became the calling places for postmen, carriers and stage coaches.

   Although Worthing's freeholders and copyholders had initially responded very cautiously to the new opportunities offered by the fashion for sea bathing, by 1790 Worthing's level sands and calm sea was already attracting 'sickly visitors'[18] and the town was described in *Topographer*[19] as being frequented by those 'who liked a more retiring bathing place than Brighton'. The potential for investing in seaside tourism rather than agriculture or fishing was now becoming more attractive to those who had surplus capital to speculate. Indeed, Richard Bacon, as both a yeoman and the proprietor of the New Inn, appears to have shown great enterprise by quickly learning the new skills that were needed when confronted with the opportunity of gaining wealth from the growing number of visitors to the hamlet who wished to immerse themselves in the sea.

   Worthing's first purpose-built lodging houses were constructed in 1794. The terrace of seven houses, later to become the northern end of Montague Place (marked 45 on Fig.49) was built on the one-and-a-half-acre enclosure called 'Drawbridge', which had been sold to John Markwick of Heene by Richard Lindup for £300.00 on the 3rd April 1792. Once acquired, John Markwick subdivided the northern end of this land parcel into seven building plots, each of which was sandwiched between a 10-ft [3.05 metre] wide carriage road constructed on the western extremity of the old enclosure and a 24-ft [7.32 metre] wide carriage road on the east. To reduce his speculative exposure, within eight months of his purchase he had sold six of the plots, retaining only one for himself. Each of the plot holders then contributed approximately £200.00 towards the cost of building the terrace of seven, three-storey red brick houses.[20] They quickly became known as the 'Seven Houses' and both Edward Snewin and Henfry Smail suggest the local inhabitants gazed in wonder at the phenomenon of seven houses built in a row.[21]

Fig. 53 *Montague Place (Spornburg)*

By 1750 terraced lodging houses were beginning to be accepted by those visiting the major spa resorts and this undoubtedly influenced speculators at both Worthing and the other emerging seaside resorts also to adopt this style of construction. Terraced property was relatively easy, cheap and quick to construct, and the rate of building could be easily regulated to reflect the demand for more or better accommodation.[22]

The residue of land between the two carriage roads that remained to the south of the original terrace of seven houses down to the sea was auctioned by John Markwick at the New Inn on the 29th August 1794 and, as can be seen from early pictures, two further terraces were constructed facing east, together with Montpelier Terrace (marked 46 on Fig. 49) at the southern end facing the sea.

It is evident from an advertisement published in the *Sussex Weekly Advertiser* dated 25th August 1794 that John Markwick also intended to sell plots for a further terrace of buildings on the eastern side of the old enclosure, facing those erected on the western side of the central carriage road. He was, however, prevailed upon by the owners of the original terrace of seven houses not to pursue this idea: they considered the open space in front of their houses should be retained as 'a railed open space of pleasure', for as such 'it would greatly increase the value of their properties and facilitate the letting of them to respectable tenants.' John Markwick appears to have conceded, for in return for a single payment of £31.00 from each of them, and their agreement to enter into a covenant to keep it as such, in perpetuity, the residue of the old enclosure became open ground, and remains as such today, although partly covered by a road.[23]

Advertisements providing the particulars of forthcoming auctions for both the sale of land and lodging houses situated at Worthing were now appearing more frequently in the *Sussex Weekly Advertiser*. At an auction held at the Sea House Inn on the 28th March 1794,

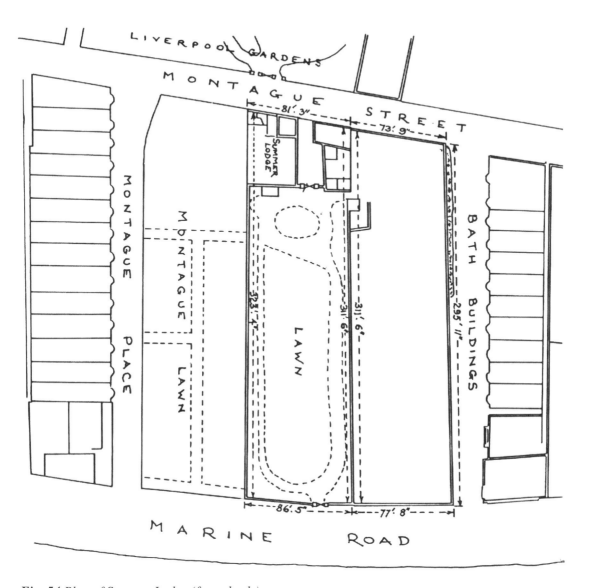

Fig. 54 *Plan of Summer Lodge (from deeds)*

'about 46 acres (customary measure) of Freehold, arable, meadow and pasture land, in
the occupation of the Rev. Mr. Whalley, a tenant at will',
was offered for sale and included in the advertisement was the observation that,
'as Worthing is now become a favourite resort of persons of the first fashion, for the
benefit of Sea Bathing, the above estate is deserving particular attention, for several
parts of it being well adapted for building on.'[24]
Thomas Richardson may well have had this potential in mind when he purchased it.[25] At
the same auction,
' A FREEHOLD, new erected Lodging House finished in the best style, and capable of
accommodating a genteel family, situate on the Sea-cliff or Terrace of Worthing, and
commanding a beautiful and extensive view of rural country and the seacoast'
was also offered for sale.[26] From the description given this would appear to be Worthing

House (marked 47 on Fig. 49) built for John Newland in 1793[27] at the junction of Chapel Road and North Street, on which Stoke Abbott Court was built in 1937.[28]

It was not only local auctions that were advertised, for in the edition of the *Sussex Weekly Advertiser* published on the 5th May 1794, an advertisement gave notice of an auction to be held by Mr. Christie in his Great Room in Pall Mall, London on the 3rd June 1794 for the sale of

'A most elegant and desirable summer residence, the property of a Nobleman ...located

at ...Worthing, twelve miles from Brighton, Sussex.'

The nobleman was the Earl of Warwick and the property was Warwick House which was purchased by J.W. Commerall, Esq.

Summer Lodge (marked 48 on Fig. 49) was erected in 1797 by Ambrose Cartwright, one of Worthing's original builders,[29] on the former old enclosure called 'Christmas Croft' (today the site of the Woolworths store on the south of Montague Street): it was immediately purchased as a summer residence by Miles Stringer, a London tea dealer.[30] The house was approached from Cross Lane (now Montague Street) by a carriage drive and its stables and coach house were located on the north-east corner of the land parcel, immediately opposite the house.[31] There was a long lawn in front of the property which extended to the foreshore, across what is now Marine Parade and the Esplanade, with only a narrow footpath between the garden and the beach. Like both Warwick House and Worthing House it was let during the season when the owner was not in residence: the more opulent visitors preferred to stay in such houses for they could then both cater for themselves and entertain. In many cases they brought with them their own servants.[32]

The popularity of Worthing had received a considerable boost when Princess Amelia, the youngest (15th) child of George III, visited Worthing in 1798 to cure a lame knee. On the advice of George III's physicians a course of seawater bathing had been prescribed and despite the hamlet's limitations and almost primitive conditions, Worthing was recommended because of its relative nearness to Windsor, good bathing at all states of the tide, and sands on which her carriage could be driven.[33] During her limited stay Miles Stringer offered the seclusion of his lawn to Princess Amelia so that she could sit in the fresh air in her chair when the state of the tide prevented her from being carried onto the beach.[34]

Unlike many of the other early seaside resorts that reaped spectacular benefits from royal patronage,[35] Worthing did not receive a comparable impact from Princess Amelia's 1798 visit: the anticipated expansion did not immediately materialise. For the town to continue growing, Worthing's early speculators needed a return on their investment in the seaside, and needed to exploit the opportunities afforded by the Napoleonic War with France which had expanded the demand for seaside holidays in England. For this to happen it was, however, essential that there was adequate road communication, allowing access from London.[36]

From at least the beginning of the eighteenth century there had been no coastal road between Worthing and Shoreham and those travelling from the north of the county had to travel on a track over the South Downs which was in part the ancient route between Arundel and Steyning.[37] Visitors travelling from London to Worthing at the end of the eighteenth century would have travelled in very uncomfortable, badly sprung, heavy vehicles with broad wheels, designed to cope with the deplorable state of the roads which were just a series of winding lanes which completely disappeared in several places.[38]

With the increase in the number of visitors to Worthing it was essential that a more direct route was established and the desired road improvement was achieved in 1804 when a direct turnpike road was opened from West Grinstead, via Washington to Worthing.[39] The Toll Gate at the Worthing end of this new turnpike road stood on the forecourt of the present Rivoli Public House and was one of three set up on the London Road, the other two

Fig. 55 *Teville Toll Gate (Nixon)*

being at Ashington and Dial Post.[40] Since coaches were always routed via turnpikes, the opening of this road provided an immediate improvement in the coach service to Worthing. Instead of there being only one coach every other weekday during the season, and a weekly wagon from London, there was now a daily service running throughout the year.[41]

Following the construction of this new turnpike road Worthing expanded very rapidly, accounting for the threefold increase in the number of houses in the Parish of Broadwater between 1801 and 1811,[42] meeting the need for additional accommodation called for by *The Times* in 1802.[43] Worthing's development was still, however, both constrained and influenced by the layout and ownership of the narrow enclosed fields that lay to the south of the large open or common fields and the farm houses and cottages of the former hamlet. The layout of the new streets and the terraces of lodging houses were dictated by the direction of the fields that preceded them. Those to the south of Warwick Street and Montague Street ran north-south, while those to the north of Warwick Street ran east-west.[44]

Although the anticipated boom following Princess Amelia's visit in 1798 did not immediately materialise it would appear that many of those owning land close to the foreshore took full advantage of the option to redeem or discharge their obligation to pay Land Tax by paying the equivalent of fifteen years' purchase in one lump sum.[45] As will be seen, their speculation was well founded, for during the first decade of the nineteenth century Worthing enjoyed a period of considerable prosperity. Several terraces of lodging houses were constructed on land adjacent to, or just a short distance from the foreshore, and once complete were immediately let at exorbitant rents.[46]

Bath Buildings, marked 49 on Fig. 49, the terrace on the eastern side of Bath Place, had been constructed by 1800 and derived its name from Wick's Baths which had been

MONTAGUE PLACE.   BATH BUILDINGS.   PARISIAN BATHS.   ROYAL SEA HOUSE H

Fig. 56 *Montague Place, Summer Lodge and Bath Buildings*

constructed on the south east corner in 1797. There were originally no houses on the west side of Bath Place, and the houses in Montague Place and Bath Place faced each other across the lawn to the south of Summer Lodge.

The name Copping's Row applied only to the row of high class lodging houses, with lawns in front, on the west side of Marine Place, marked 50 on Fig.49. They were named after John Copping, a carpenter, and were crowded with fashionable visitors during the season. To the north of Copping's Row were stables, while the southern end was always known as Marine Place.

The ancient three-acre enclosure, known as South Lands, which adjoined the rear of the properties on the eastern side of Marine Place had been sold by Mary Morris following her marriage to William Wicks in 1794. The ancient 'Capital Messuage' South House, which had stood for centuries at the northern end, was demolished and the land was subdivided into building plots. The first of the plots to be sold were at the south-eastern end of this land parcel immediately adjoining the sea. They were purchased by William Hall, a Brighthelmstone (Brighton) bricklayer, who erected the three houses known as Little Terrace (marked 51 on Fig.49).[47]

Bedford Row (marked 52 on Fig.49), a terrace of four-storey yellow brick lodging houses, with curved bay windows rising through their full height, overlooked Bedford Lawn to the east and had been erected on this land parcel by 1803. The two lodging houses, inappropriately named as Great Terrace (marked 53 on Fig.49) located at the southern end of Bedford Row, facing the sea, had been constructed by 1804. At the northern end of Bedford Row were stables and coach houses and access to Warwick Street was through a stable yard.[48] John Evans records in the town's first guide book, written in 1804, that

Fig. 57 *Little and Great Terrace*

Fig. 58 *Bedford House*

'Montague Place and Bedford Row constitute the longest range of buildings ... and both of them form conspicuous objects near the foreshore. They rear their fronts with a neatness and elegance, which render them appropriate habitations for persons of fortune and respectability. Although raised at different periods they vie with each other in the beauty of their prospects and in the salubrity of their situations.'[49]

By 1805 it would appear that there was accommodation 'suitable to every class of visitor'.[50] Some houses were 'sufficiently commodious to be fit for families of the first distinction'. Both Summer Lodge and Warwick House were let during the 'season'. Worthing House, owned by John Newland, Esq., 'at the entrance to the hamlet on the traveller's approach towards the town' was also let as a lodging house and 'accommodated with ease a large family'.[51] Bedford House (marked 54 on Fig. 49), situated immediately to the east of Bedford Row with an unrestricted view of the sea, was also let to visitors during the season. It had been built in c. 1790 by Thomas Lane, of Hampton Court,[52] on the small copyhold enclosure that was part of the 'demesne' land of the 'reputed manor of Sheep-combe' in Findon, which had been held by the Vicars Choral of Chichester Cathedral from at least 1631.

Fig. 59 *Worthing seafront (Nixon)*

An acceptable, but standardised, social routine had been formulated at the eighteenth-century spa resorts and this had been transformed with very little modification to the formality of the emerging 'fashionable coastal watering places'. Having found suitable lodgings, visitors to Worthing were soon integrated into the daily pattern of the Georgian resort routine. The day began with sea bathing or a visit to the warm baths before breakfast.[53] During the day they visited one of the libraries to read the newspapers or took further exercise, watched the pony and donkey racing on the beach, or played cricket on the Downs.[54] The less energetic just strolled on Worthing's extensive sandy beach, described by Evans as being 'as smooth as a carpet and level as a lawn'.[55] Pleasure boats were also available in which 'for a few shillings' the more adventurous could 'be wafted along the coast in safety'. Visitors also expected to be able to admire views, go riding on the Downs and to visit country houses, and the Sussex coastline offered the climate and scenic variety that was expected.[57] In the evenings most visitors again visited the libraries to indulge in a mild game of loo, with music and a lottery as added distractions. The beach, bathing machines and seawater baths were, however, the distinctive novelties of the seaside.[58] The first priority of almost every visitor was access to the sea, to bathe, promenade or just to inhale the ozone.[59]

Fig. 60 *Wick's Warm Baths*

Warm baths of varying degrees of luxury were erected at most of the emerging watering places as these were essential for maintaining the 'salt water cure' during either the winter or inclement weather. Wicks' Original Royal Baths, marked 55 on Fig.49, located just west of the modern Arcade at the southern end of Bath Place, were opened in 1797 by John Wicks, one of Worthing's earliest resident entrepreneurs.[60] The small single-storeyed wooden building, which projected some distance in front of the building line,[61] had been strategically sited so as to minimise the length of pipe through which the seawater was pumped to the baths. According to John Evans, the seawater could be heated to whatever temperature was desired, 'thus ensuring that the benefit of cold and hot water bathing, so much insisted upon by the faculty, could be enjoyed in perfection.'[62] These remained as Worthing's only hot seawater baths until 1818, when Thomas Trotter built the Royal Baths at Marlborough House, located in Marine Parade on the corner of Paragon Street.[63] These later became Henney's Royal Baths and then the Marlborough Hotel (demolished in 1940).[64]

Although sea bathing was supposed to be enjoyable as well as medically beneficial, the activity was still very primitive. Many gentlemen still bathed naked from a boat or the

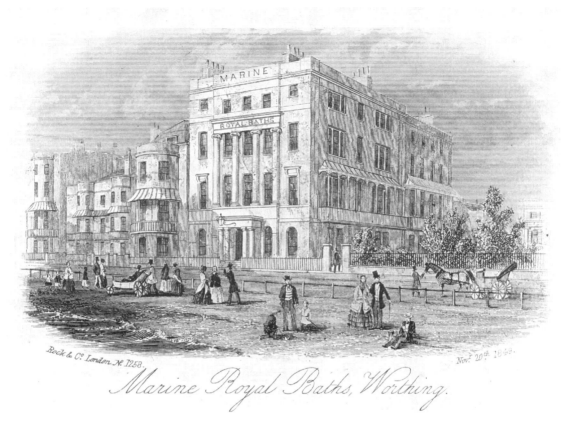

Fig. 61 *Royal Baths, Marlborough Place*

beach, while the ladies disrobed in a little hut before plunging into the sea wrapped in voluminous and nondescript garments.

By the beginning of the nineteenth century most resorts had a collection of bathing machines for visitors' use. Bathing machines are recorded at Worthing from as early as 1789,[65] and their number had increased from about thirty in 1804 to over sixty by 1813.[66] The cost for using a bathing machine was 'one shilling for each individual and sixpence for children under seven years of age'.[67] This room on wheels was dragged out into the water by a horse and in theory provided the privacy of an indoor bathing establishment - and no lady would have considered bathing without its protective presence. Unless one was lucky enough to get it early in the day, the bathing machine was a very unattractive object: damp, ill-lit, ill-ventilated, its floor covered with sand and seawater which had dripped from its previous occupants or perhaps even sloshed up the steps of the machine while it was out in the sea. It was set in motion as soon as its hirer was inside and the occupant had to change into her bathing costume as best she could in such a confined space while the machine jolted and shook its way down the beach and into the water.[69]

For decades, the bathing machines and their notorious attendants ruled the visitor's sea. Sea bathing was looked upon as a nauseous dose and because of this, a new profession, the dipper, came in to being to assist the reluctant bathers. While it often required the effort of two or more stalwart 'longshoremen' to duck the gentlemen bathers a stout and fantastically garbed old woman of the Martha Gunn type officiated for ladies.[69] Having partaken of their nauseous dose they had to return into the bathing machine to dry themselves and change out of their costume - again whilst it was in motion.

Anyone entering the sea at Worthing during the first half of the nineteenth century had every reason to be reluctant, for there had not been any real attempt to provide a piped drainage system to serve the town. Total reliance had been placed on an antiquated and primitive network of ditches that discharged straight into the sea. Often these ditches carried both surface water and sewerage, even though this was forbidden by the 'Town Act' of 1803. As the health and comfort of visitors was an essential part of any resort's stock in trade it seems inconceivable that, in a town whose continued expansion depended entirely on its popularity as a health and holiday resort, these ditches were allowed to discharge their noxious contents among the bathers, leaving rivulets of sewage on the beach as the tide receded.

It was not only sewage that dissuaded the more enlightened, for in a letter written by the Bishop of Lichfield and Coventry to Admiral Cornwallis in 1811 the bishop remarks,

'Worthing seems to be a most excellent place for sea-bathing: but the sea-weed thrown up by the tide over the sands is so offensive that I shall never willingly frequent it.'

Although considered by many to be a twentieth-century phenomenon, the problem of seaweed being driven on shore is recorded as early as 1805[70] and in December 1828 the Town Commissioners ordered proceedings to be taken against anyone depositing 'seaweed in heaps on the sea-beach', apparently under the impression that the manifestation was the work of some ill-disposed persons working under the cover of darkness.[71]

Like the eighteenth-century spas, the emerging nineteenth-century seaside resorts had to cater for seekers of pleasure, recreation, novelty and status as well as those purely seeking health and rest. Whilst a small minority of the visitors preferred quiet and seclusion, most wanted artificial amusements and opportunities for carefully regulated social mixing.[72] The early promoters of the resort had been local men, such as members of the Bacon and Wicks families. By 1800 they had been joined by outsiders notably William France, upholsterer to the King, who built the first lodging houses in Trafalgar Place, and Edward Ogle, a wealthy London stockbroker and landowner from Clapham, who had purchased the various parcels of land that then comprised the Warwick House Estate from Major William Commerall in 1801.[73]

Investment in the provision of the specialist resort functions found at all the established spa resorts, however, required a much larger capital investment and a specialist knowledge of the fashionable clientele's needs if they were to be successful.[74] As a former London stockbroker, Edward Ogle would have experienced polite society at least in London, if not at a spa town, and would have known that Worthing's growth beyond its limited early expansion as a resort was conditional on the further provision of institutions and entertainments which were already firmly established in the urban culture of the provinces, as well as that of London and the spa towns.

Within a year of acquiring the Warwick House Estate, Edward Ogle had arranged for The Colonnade (marked 56 on Fig.59) to be constructed at the junction of Warwick Street and High Street, immediately opposite Warwick House. As the engraving dated 1804 (reproduced as Figure 62) reveals, The Colonnade clearly complemented the architecture of Warwick House. It was a unified and graceful building with an attractive curved arcade, decorated with cast-iron balustrades running around the raised ground floor and approached at each end by steps. At first-floor level cast-iron balconies echoed the balustrades of the ground floor.[75]

Numbers 1, 2 and 3 The Colonnade, approached from High Street up stone steps, were all lodging houses, number 3 having been sold to Mary Lindup on the 23rd September 1803.[76] The southern end of the building, facing Warwick Street, was let by William Ogle

Fig.62 *Warwick House and Colonnade Library (1804)*

to Mary Spooner as a Circulating Library and it is obvious from the architectural enhancements to this end of the building that Edward Ogle had considered such a use when formulating the design.

The spa towns had provided a successful model for the entertainment of the upper and prosperous middle ranks of society, the very clientele that Edward Ogle was trying to attract to the town. Emulating the spa towns, all the resorts that were already firmly established, such as Brighton and Margate, had a circulating library with an adjoining coffee and newspaper room, for these libraries had become the dominant social institutions of the seaside. Jane Austen's novels show just how important libraries were as meeting places. Subscribers signed the visitors' book to record their subscription but, more importantly, to announce their arrival to others who might call into the library to read, exchange gossip, gamble or to listen to the musical entertainments that were performed in the evening.[78]

During the first decade of the nineteenth century the Colonnade Library was regarded as a major improvement in the amenities provided at Worthing and very quickly became the rendezvous for the fashionable visitors to the town.[79] In addition to having access to an extensive reading room, where new works of fiction, the latest works on sea bathing and the most popular of the London papers were available, visitors were able to enter lotteries and play games like Loo. Tunbridge ware, cheap jewellery and other trinkets were also offered for sale.[80]

By 1808, Worthing had expanded sufficiently to become a Post Town and Mrs. Spooner became the town's first postmaster, earning a yearly salary of £101-16s-4d. Prior to that letters had to be sent

> 'to the Post Town of Shoreham, the postmaster of which place will convey them to Worthing and a Mr. Stafford, who keeps a circulating library at Worthing, will receive and deliver them for one penny per letter'.[81]

Worthing's first circulating library had been established by a Mr. Burke, prior to 1798, at the southern end of Marine Place. This may have been taken over by Mr. Stafford,

Fig. 63 *Stafford's New Marine Library*

for there is a reference to Stafford's Old Library being in the same location before he opened, prior to 1805, his new fashionable premises, marked 57 on Fig.49, immediately to the west of the Steyne Hotel.[82] When originally designed by the architect John Rebecca, both Stafford's Marine Library and the adjoining property (Rebecca House) were flat fronted with a balcony at first floor level over a veranda below. In 1817 a letter was sent to the Town Commissioners by T. Eadison, Esq. on behalf of the residents of Bedford Row,

> 'Complaining that dancing and quarrelling at Stafford's Old Library continually kept
> them up at night to their very great nuisance.'

In response the Town Commissioners requested the landlord, Mr. Thomas Bushby, to use his influence to try and abate the nuisance, otherwise 'they would be obliged to have it indicted as a disorderly house'.[83]

As only a minority of the early nineteenth-century visitors placed a resort's natural attributes above all other considerations, a prerequisite for Worthing's continuing success was the ability to cater for those who sought entertainment. Although the Worthing area had been visited for many years by itinerant bands of players who performed from temporary booths, it was not until 1802 that the first indoor theatrical performance was given by Thomas Trotter, an actor manager, and his company in a barn in High Street. Performances at this barn-theatre were, however, limited to a three-month summer season of August to October, when it was open on a Monday, Wednesday and Friday.[84] Despite its undoubted discomfort and unsuitability it appears to have secured some measure of patronage for the following 34 residents signed a petition dated 29th June 1803 advocating the construction of a permanent purpose-built theatre.[83]

Edward Ogle
Michael Morrah
Edward Hide
John Isaacs
Henry Phillips
William Wicks
Mary Spooner
Andras Rencketts
Richard Palmer
Susan Bloss
Charles Viner
John Barker

Mary Smith
John Wicks
John Marshall
John Snelling
John Hide
Edward Stanford
James Smith
G. Deadman
T.C.Moore
Ambrose Cartwright
James Sewell

Richard Smith
George Wingfield Jnr.
Hannah Brown
Mrs Burford
Thomas Shotter
John Markwick
David Thomas
Mrs Shotter
John Cadmington
John Rogers
Edward Rogers

They were all

'Of the opinion that respectable theatrical representations would add to the interest of this place and being destitute of any amusement will be acceptable to visitors. Mr Trotter being well recommended, we give him the preference to any other manner and acquiesce in establishing a theatre.'[86]

The first signatory on the petition was that of Edward Ogle, who following discussions with Thomas Trotter in the October of 1803, provided the finance for the construction of Worthing's first permanent theatre on land he owned on the northern side of Ann Street. For Edward Ogle it was his most speculative venture at Worthing, for the success of the theatre was totally dependent on Thomas Trotter, whom he had appointed as its manager. As the theatre was only licensed for performances on sixty nights in a summer season that ran from July to October, for Edward Ogle to see a return on his money it was essential that Trotter was able to attract good players and choose programmes that would fill the theatre to capacity at most of the performances in order that there was a profit after he had paid his employees and kept the equipment and costumes in good order.[87]

The theatre, marked 58 on Fig.49, designed by Edward Hide, was like most of the Georgian resort theatres.[87] Its exterior was quite simple and plain and when first constructed did not have the four columns and covered way that is shown on all the surviving photographs or the parapet walls that were subsequently constructed to hide the roof. In direct contrast, the interior, which was constructed in the shape of a horseshoe, was quite lavish. It had a capacity of between six and seven hundred people. There was a dress circle with three tiers of seats, upper boxes and four private boxes, together with five higher and lower boxes, pit and gallery. The pit (where the audience stood) extended right up to the orchestra. The fronts of the boxes, the ceiling and the proscenium had all been handsomely decorated by G. Francis Williams, a scenic artist from Drury Lane, London, who had also been commissioned to design and construct the scenery. Around the boxes were seven glass chandeliers which had cost £98.0s.0d. These were lit with wax candles, while the lamps in other parts of the theatre were lit with oil. A large scene room was provided, in which a considerable amount of scenery and several drop scenes were stored. Over the scenic room was the wardrobe in which the costumes were kept. The dressing rooms were behind the stage, each having a large fireplace which must have made them very comfortable. The investment had, however, been considerable. The construction of the theatre had cost £6,992-2s-0d; scenery, machinery, flies, furniture, wardrobe, music, chandeliers, printed play books, manuscripts and sundries added a further £1,547-4s-0d, making a total of £8,539-6s-6d.[88]

The opening of the theatre took place on the 7th July 1807, when a capacity audience saw a performance of the *Merchant of Venice* and a farce entitled *Children in the Wood*. The theatre's first season was very successful. Under the able management of Thomas

Fig. 64 Sketch of the Ann Street theatre as originally built in c. *1807*

Trotter, many of the most popular players of the day, either recruited from the London theatres or who later made a name for themselves as stars at Drury Lane or Govent Garden, played to capacity audiences which included many of the notable visitors to the town.[89] The cost of admission to the stage boxes, which were carpeted and provided with a pier mirror and cane-seated chairs, was two guineas, the dress circle was five shillings, the upper circle three shillings and six pence, the pit half a crown, and the gallery a shilling. As the theatre had a capacity of between six to seven hundred people for each performance, and good houses produced as much as £100 per night (very similar to the return achieved at the theatre at Brighton) there was a potential return of approximately £6,000.0s.0d per year. Despite, or possibly because of the great success of the first season, in true entrepreneurial style, on the 4th February 1808 Edward Ogle sold both the theatre and the land that adjoined it to Thomas Trotter for the sum of £2,620.0s.0d.. Edward Ogle was, therefore, totally recompensed for his insight and courage for investing in this particular essential seaside amenity.[90]

     Although many speculators had invested in the provision of lodging houses and Edward Ogle had ensured that the more important of the amenities found at the spa resorts had been emulated at Worthing, the provision of hotel accommodation still remained very inadequate. Edward Snewin records in his reminiscences 'when the town was suddenly called upon to accommodate an influx of visitors' on the 17th August 1805, that 'only twenty-seven of the party were able to dine at the Sea House Inn and fifteen at the New Inn'. Other than a further 'one or two who managed to get accommodation at the Nelson Inn' the majority had to return to Brighton hungry.[91]

     The situation clearly did not go unnoticed, for the Steyne Hotel, marked 59 on fig.49, was opened on the 1st July 1807 at the southern end of the one-acre freehold land parcel

Fig. 65 *Steyne Hotel*

Edward Ogle had acquired when he purchased the Warwick House estate in 1801. Yet again using his entrepreneurial skill, he invested in both its construction and management, holding ten out of the sixteen shares.[92] It immediately satisfied the requirement for a first-class hotel to satisfy the needs of the increasing number of fashionable visitors to the town and its assembly room became the social centre of the resort.[93] On the ground floor was an elegant public coffee room with handsome sitting rooms, as well as the private rooms and offices of the household. Over these was a ballroom with card rooms and other numerous suites of apartments 'in the first degree of elegance'.[94]

To the north of the Steyne Hotel, on the same land parcel, Edward Ogle also allowed a terrace of twenty-three four-storey dwelling houses to be constructed by 1808, and, again as a true entrepreneur, retained the ownership of numbers 14, 15 and 23.[95] Known as 'The New Steyne', marked 60 on fig. 49, they were unmistakably part of his overall strategy to attract fashionable visitors to the resort. Stafford's Guide, published in 1810, suggests

> 'the upper apartments of these houses ...afford prospects to the line of coast east-wards as far as Shoreham, Brighton, the clifted promontories of Rottingdean, Seaford and Beachy Head; they are also well situated for sea views and are likewise at an agreeable distance from the bathing places, libraries and promenade of the company.'[96]

Both the Steyne Hotel and this terrace of dwelling houses overlooked Steyne Gardens, which was then, like today, a public garden surrounded by trees. This was again land owned by Edward Ogle, and by laying it out as a pleasure garden, modelled on the Steyne at Brighton, he had ensured that the view to the south from Warwick House would never be obstructed or diminished in any way. The owners of the houses overlooking the Steyne had a right of access to these gardens and each house paid one guinea a year towards their upkeep. As the general public also had the use of these gardens they obtained very little, if any, advantage for their outlay.[97]

Fig. 66 *The Steyne from the north*

Within eight years of acquiring the Warwick House estate, Edward Ogle (known in the locality as 'King Ogle' because of his autocratic behaviour) had achieved his aim, emulation of the model provided by the spas for the entertainment of the upper and prosperous middle ranks of society. Facilities were now available for assemblies, for dancing and cards, which together with the circulating library and the coffee house provided the formal and exclusive institutions that dominated 'visitor society' until the early railway age. There was, however, one subtle difference: entry to the charmed circle of the 'company' at the seaside resorts, as defined by participation in the round of balls, card parties, raffles and public assemblies that made up the season, was regrettably not afforded by social status, but by an ability to pay the expensive subscriptions and participation fees.[98]

While the late eighteenth- and early-nineteenth century entrepreneurs and speculators had ensured that Worthing had sufficient lodging houses and all the essential resort amenities there was no local government machinery capable of dealing with the problems arising from its rapid growth into a fashionable[99] resort. The narrow, dirty and unpaved lanes that had previously only had to serve a small hamlet were quite unsuitable for the quality of visitor Worthing was now attracting, and its sanitary facilities were totally inadequate. The majority of its effluent was still discharged onto the beach indiscriminately for the tides to clear away via a network of open sewers or ditches which for centuries had only been required to drain and discharge surface water from the fields to the south of the ancient footpath to Heene, which later became Richmond Road.

Worthing was still governed as part of the ecclesiastical and civil parish of Broadwater. In theory Worthing's inhabitants in partnership with those at Broadwater were totally responsible for the conduct of parish affairs and the inadequate development of Worthing's infrastructure was a direct result of the limited finance and out-dated administrative powers of the Broadwater vestry. Some measure of independent authority was, therefore, essential if the investment made by the early promoters of the resort was to be protected by Worthing continuing to develop into a 'fashionable Georgian watering place'.

Instigated by the early promoters of the resort[100] and supported by the local gentry, the desired authority was achieved in 1803 when an Act of Parliament was passed separating Worthing from Broadwater for the purpose of civil administration. The Act, known as the 'Worthing Town Act',[101] entrusted the administration of the town to a Board of Commissioners who were given powers to safeguard the interests of the inhabitants. Although seventy-two names were nominated in the Act, with powers to replace themselves by co-option, only seven were needed to form a quorum and rarely did more than twelve take an active part in the town's administration.[102] The Commissioners were empowered to levy a paving rate of not more than 2s-6d (12.5p) in the pound on the security of which they were able to borrow up to £2,000.[103] There was also a controversial provision that empowered the Commissioners to claim a proportionate part of the Highway and Surveyors Rate levied by Broadwater Parish vestry for the maintenance of the roads in the town and this caused numerous disputes between the Commissioners and the Broadwater Vestry.[104] With this revenue they were required to adequately drain the town, purchase a fire engine, establish a police force and construct properly paved, lit and cleansed streets. The preamble to the Act stated that the hamlet of Worthing should in future be known as the 'Town of Worthing'. This would appear to have been only a courtesy title initially for the total population of the Parish of Broadwater, which included Worthing, was in 1801 only 1018.[106]

As most of the active Commissioners were either local businessmen or tradesmen, they usually held their meetings in the evening. The first meeting was held at the Nelson Inn in South Street on the 13th June 1803 under the chairmanship of Edward Ogle, who naturally wished to take a leading part in the administration of the town, if only to protect his considerable investment in its resort amenities! Mr. George Mant was appointed as clerk and was paid one guinea for each meeting he attended. Dr. Michael Morrah, one of Worthing's first doctors, was appointed treasurer and Edward Paine, beadle, town crier and rate collector. The beadle's salary was fixed at ten pounds a year in addition to half a guinea every time he summoned the Commissioners to a meeting and a commission of sixpence in the pound on the rates he collected.[106] A surveyor of drains, later of drains and roads, was appointed in 1804, but was apparently unpaid until 1822. For the use of his premises the landlord at the Nelson Inn, Edmund Blann, was paid half a guinea each time his room was used.[107] The Commissioners continued to meet at the Nelson Inn until the 14th February 1812 when they changed their venue to The Royal George in Market Street. As required by the Act, the Commissioners immediately set out new streets, improved the existing ones and laid covered drains in place of the open ditches that had previously served this purpose.[108]

Early guide books describe the town as being fresh and bright, with terraces of cream brick, as yet unweathered, and smaller houses of red and black bricks or flints. Its initial development had, however, been limited to the very narrow tract of land to the south of Warwick Street and was a distinct cluster of properties to the south of both the ancient common or open fields and the old farm houses and cottages of the hamlet, and many of the newly formed gravelled roads disconcertingly ended in either a field or market garden. It would appear that this distinction between the newly emerging town and the ancient hamlet was clearly evident to John Evans, for when describing Worthing House he suggests it was 'at the entrance of the village...on the approach to the town after passing the toll bar'.[109]

It is evident that the improvements in the town's infrastructure, implemented by the newly appointed Board of Commissioners, were sufficient for Worthing to continue to develop, for between 1803 and 1808 substantial houses were built on the land formerly owned by Edward Ogle on the northern side of Warwick Street from the Colonnade Library at its eastern end to Brook Street (later South Place) in the west. In all the emerging Georgian seaside resorts the perceived development potential of the sub-divided building plots was totally dependent upon their size, location and depth and it would appear that Edward Ogle deliberately sub-divided this former ancient parcel of enclosed land into narrow but deep building plots that ran north–south for its entire width.[110] By creating these deep and narrow building plots, with his usual entrepreneurial skill he was able to fully exploit the valuable main street frontage adjoining Warwick Street by selling it off for either residential properties or lodging houses, while utilising the residual land to the rear for cheaper housing, workshops, yards and mews. He was able to do this because the essential rear access to serve the residual 'back land' already existed on the adjoining land parcel to the north also owned by him. Running along the southern boundary of 'Mole Soals,' which Edward Ogle had acquired as part of the Warwick House estate, was a track way which for many years had been used for access to both the adjoining land on the south and a granary and stables that had been built on this old enclosure prior to 1801. By 1805 this track way had become 'a street or road called or intended to be called Ann Street', named after Edward Ogle's wife.[111] It was not, however, until the meeting of Worthing's Town Commissioners held on the 11th September 1809 that Ann Street was considered and deemed a Public Highway.[112]

Before the completion of the southern end of Chapel Road in 1816, Brook Street (later South Place), which had also been laid out as a road prior to 1805, was the only entry into Ann Street and this may well account for its initial importance.[113] The name Brook Street did not survive for many years, for by 1814 it had changed to South Place. Although the road disappeared when the modern Guildbourne Centre was constructed, the name can still be clearly seen on the HSBC Bank building on the north-west corner of Warwick Street, next to the pedestrian approach from Warwick Street to the Guildbourne Centre

Fig. 67 *Early view of Warwick Street from the east*

entrance. When looking at the northern side of Warwick Street today (marked 61 on Fig. 49) it is difficult to comprehend that nearly all the buildings were initially either substantial residential properties or lodging houses, patronised by the increasing number of fashionable visitors to the town. All the original ground floor facades have been displaced by modern shop fronts and signage, but above these a few of the original curved bay windows and the occasional original yellow brick facade with classical window heads can still be seen. Interspersed amongst them, were, however, some of Worthing's first commercial properties and shops.[114] Unlike those of today, most were crude conversions of the original residential property. Many retained their ground floor bow windows and were approached from the street up the stone steps that had originally been used when they were private houses.[115]

Early nineteenth-century rate books reveal the houses on the northern side of

Warwick Street were originally numbered consecutively, starting at the eastern end.[116] Residing at No.5 [today No.37] was John Lipscombe, a hairdresser, and at No.7 [today No.33] Samuel Stubbs, a baker, whose oven and bakehouse was immediately to the rear of his house. The water supply to all the houses near the sea had the reputation of being brackish, and to overcome this Mr Stubbs advertised on his business cards 'Free access to Stubbs pump of excellent water'.[117] John Snelling, a shoemaker, lived at No.9 [today No.29] and No.13 [today No.21] was a large grocer's shop owned by Mr. Charles Viner, which was approached up a flight of stairs. Mr. John Joanes, a stonemason, resided at No.16 [today No.15]. Immediately behind,

Fig. 68 43 Warwick Street prior to conversion

fronting onto Ann Street, was his stonemason's yard and workshops. William Munday, Worthing's first 'chemist and druggist', resided at No.18 [today No.11]. Mr. Thomas Shotter, a saddler and harness maker, occupied No.20 [today No.7].[118] This property had a little gallery in front with steps at each end and an iron rail on which, according to Edward Snewin, Mr. Shotter used to hang saddles and harnesses.[119] The design of the facade of this building, was, until its unsympathetic conversion in the early 1960's, considered to be one of Worthing's finest examples of Georgian architecture and was almost certainly designed by John Rebecca. The principal draper's of the emerging town was kept by Mr. Christopher Taylor, who resided at No.22 [today No.3].

Early rate books also reveal that in many cases the less fashionable property constructed on the residual land to the rear, fronting Ann Street, was rated with its counterpart in Warwick Street. Joseph Ediston had a cabinet maker's shop to the rear of No.3 [today No.41] which was a lodging house let out in season by Dr. Michael Morrah who was 'highly spoken of by visitors' as being 'distinguished for his surgical skill'.[120] There was another workshop to the rear of No.8 [today No.31] owned by Thomas Palmer, a plumber and glazier, and to the rear of numbers 14 and 15 [today 19 and 17 Warwick Street] was 'Toogoods Passage'. This was a terrace of four small lower-class dwellings that faced west, their only outlook being the side wall of a coach-house and stable owned by Thomas Trotter. Both William Toogood and Henry Berry, the town's two principal donkey and pony proprietors, resided here. Edward Snewin records that

> 'William Toogood did a roaring trade during the season, and that he was known to treat his donkeys kindly in an age that was not noted for its humanity to animals.'[121]

Fig. 69 *Early picture of South Street* (c. *1820)*

By 1804 most of the properties on the east side of South Street (marked 62 on fig.49) had been constructed on the former old enclosure called 'pond croft' and according to early guide books were either 'occupied by persons in business' or were 'lodging houses of a second fashion'.[122] When originally constructed nearly all the properties had bow-faced facades,[123] but most have been entirely obliterated by modern development. The booking offices for the various stage coaches that conveyed Worthing's pre-Victorian visitors to the town were all situated at the southern end of South Street. In 1805 coaches from London ran from the Golden Cross, Charing Cross on Monday, Wednesday and Friday and from the Spread Eagle, Gracechurch Street, on Tuesdays, Thursdays and Saturdays, leaving at seven in the morning.[124]

Properties had also been built by 1805 on either side of Chapel Street (today Portland Road) which prior to the implementation of the enclosure act only extended from Montague Street to the southern end of the West Field. This newly created road derived its name from the small Independent Dissenting Chapel (marked 63 on fig.49) which had been erected in 1804[125] on the corner of Portland Road and Montague Street, the site of the modern Boots store.

The influx of fashionable visitors to the town had provided direct employment for dressmakers, shoemakers, milliners and jewellers. Catering for their culinary needs had also provided employment for butchers, bakers and confectioners. John Evans records that by 1805

> 'shops filled with articles well assorted for a family, and of the best quality are to be found here of nearly every description…The increase of visitors and consequently of inhabitants has occasioned an adequate supply of beef, veal, pork, South Down mutton, lamb and poultry of all kinds, on reasonable terms. Here are also vegetables of all sorts of profusion…The fish are very fine. The beautiful silver mackrael are caught on this coast; and the quantity often seen poured out on the beach, cannot fail to excite our admiration. The shrimps are of a very fine flavour and when eaten almost immediately after they are taken out of the sea, they may be reckoned a real delicacy. Lobsters and crabs are caught here as well as brought from Bognor Rocks; they are exceedingly fresh and of course pleasant to the taste, a circumstance of which a person ever so partial to fish of this kind, who has never visited the sea-side, can form no conception'.[126]

Private banks had also increased in number between 1797 and 1810 and many, like those established at Worthing, were set up by groups of local businessmen to provide finance for commercial expansion. The Worthing Bank was located in the large corner building at the northern end of the Steyne (marked 64 on fig.49) that is today Whibley's the Jewellers.[127] This building had been erected in c. 1807/8 in the distinctive yellow brick used in many of the more fashionable buildings of this period. The Worthing Bank was underwritten by the London bankers, Messrs. Ramsbottom and Newman, and the Worthing partners were Samuel Hawkins and Henry Phillips. Like most of the banks established at the beginning of the nineteenth century they issued their own bank notes, as those of the Bank of England rarely circulated much beyond London and coinage was in short supply due to the constant threat of invasion throughout the prolonged Napoleonic wars with France between 1793 and 1815.[128]

Fig. 70 *Bank note for £1.0s.0d issued by the Worthing Bank*

Banking during the unsettled Napoleonic period was a precarious business: many of these early local banks were very susceptible to financial failure, often from a single bad debt,[129] and it would appear that this particular bank had 'failed' by 1811.[130] Although the property was still referred to as the Old Bank until at least 1828, rate books reveal that Mr. Summerton Bennett paid the rates from 1822. Edward Snewin, in his reminiscences of old Worthing, recalls that the 'Old Bank premises' were converted into a grocer's shop by Mr. Summerton Bennett and the bank safe remained in the property for many years.[131]

Henty's Bank (marked 65 on fig.49) originally known as the 'Worthing and Sussex Bank' when established in 1808, was located in the yellow brick building that is today the Vintners Parrott on the corner of Warwick Street and Bedford Row, and the name 'Bank Chambers' can still be seen over its former entrance in Bedford Row.[132] It was very much a family enterprise. The first partners were Thomas Henty, who farmed 284 acres at West Tarring, his brother George, a Mr. Oliver who was a maternal relative, a Mr. Hopkins, who was a nearby landowner and a relation of Thomas Henty's wife, and Colonel Margesson, the owner of Offington Manor and Thomas Henty's senior officer in the County Yeomanry. Like the Worthing Bank it was also part financed by the issue of notes to the value of £1.0.0d, £2.0.0d, £5.0.0d and £10.0.0d.[133] William Margesson resigned from the partnership in 1816 and Mr. George Henty became senior partner. Mr. Edward Upperton of Thakeham joined the partnership a year or two later.[134]

Fig. 71 Bank note for £5.0s.0d issued by the Worthing and Sussex Bank

Following the defeat of Napoleon a wave of financial instability broke over the whole country. Sixty banks failed nation wide and Sussex was badly affected. As most of the early local banks only served a relatively small area they were very susceptible to the vagaries of the economy and those located in the emerging Georgian seaside watering places were especially vulnerable. The Worthing and Sussex Bank survived, possibly because Mr. George Henty and his partners had the foresight to widen the bank's business catchment area, having opened branches at Horsham and Thakeham as separate undertakings, each with their own note issue, thus diversifying the potential financial risk. Henty's Bank, after having been run by the same family for nearly ninety years, was incorporated in 1896 into the Capital and Counties Bank which merged with Lloyds Bank in 1917.[135]

The rapid increase in population and associated prosperity in aspiring fashionable seaside resorts like Worthing created a demand, not only for the obvious resort facilities like accommodation, baths and libraries, but also the other basic and essential requirements of any other rapidly expanding Georgian town; stables and mews for horses, coaches and wagons. Although there were isolated stables in most parts of Worthing in the first decade of the nineteenth century, information from deeds suggest that there had been a conscious decision to locate the majority of the commercial stables and associated trades of carriers, blacksmiths and coach builders in the relatively small and compact area between Ann Street and Cook's Row (modern Chatsworth Road).

The town's first commercial stables (marked 67 on fig. 49) were located at the western end of Ann Street on a plot of land that had formerly been part of the old enclosure called 'Mole Soals'. It had been sold by Edward Ogle for £500.00 in January 1805 to James Constable, an Arundel builder, and three Arundel brewers, Edward Puttock, Thomas Constable and his brother George.[136] Being directly to the north of the newly constructed Brook Street (later South Place), which at the time provided the only access into Ann Street, these commercial entrepreneurs clearly saw the potential of the location and constructed a cottage, a stable that could accommodate forty horses and coach houses on the land acquired by them.[137] Land Tax records reveal that from c. 1808 to 1814 the occupier of these stables was Thomas Harding[138] and on Phillips' map dated 1814 these premises are named as Nelson Mews, no doubt to commemorate Lord Nelson who died at the Battle of Trafalgar on the 21st October 1805. The selection of the word 'mews' rather than stable is very apt as the original definition of 'mews' is a small street behind a residential street containing private stables for the town's houses.[139]

Immediately to the east of Nelson Mews were the stables and premises of George Mant (marked 68 on fig.49). This stable complex, only 26 feet [7.92 metres] wide had been built between 1805 and 1809 and was occupied by John Giddington. By 1811 John Joanes had taken over the premises,[140] which are still shown as stables on Phillips' map of 1814. Within a year the stables had been converted to a brewery as can be seen from the Town Commissioners' minute of 15th May 1815 when it was ordered,

> 'that the clerk do proceed to indict John Joanes of Worthing, Brewer, for the nuisance to the Public by the foul and waste water thrown from his Brewhouse unless the said John Joanes shall make a proper drain to carry off such foul and waste water into the main drain of the Town of Worthing'.

At first there was no accommodation for drinking on the premises and, according to Snewin, the thirsty ones used to stand on the pavement outside and drink their beer. After the passing of the Beer Act in 1830, a tap and smoking room was provided. It later became a meeting place of the more Liberal and Radical element in the town and became known as the 'Reform Club'.[141]

By the end of 1809 a further stable (marked 69 on Fig. 49) had been erected for the Steyne Hotel on land that had been conveyed to John Penfold of Goring, yeoman, by Edward and James Ogle for £630.[142] The Ann Street entrance was a central archway. There were lofts and sleeping accommodation over the front bays known as the 'soldiers rooms', probably commemorating billeting during the French invasion scare.[143] To the north of these stables was the old enclosed parcel of land known as 'Long Garden', the major part of which had been purchased in 1808 from George Newland by Richard Cook of Worthing, a builder.[144] A piece of this land, abutting the northern boundary of the Steyne Stables, was sold by Cook to James Penfold in December 1809.[145] He erected several coach houses and stables together with other buildings and offices on the site and on 12th July 1810 conveyed the premises to Edward Ogle for £1650. Edward Ogle subsequently let these premises to George Parsons, owner of the Steyne Hotel, who added it to his own adjoining stables and premises fronting Ann Street. Phillips' map of 1814 shows entrances existed at both the Market Street and Ann Street ends of the amalgamated properties.

In 1825 Mr. John Snewin purchased the eastern portion of these stables and erected a carpenter's shop, timber shed and saw pit. The western portion of the stables was sub-let to Richard Robinson, carrier, who following the death of his father in 1823, had transferred his family business to this location from its former site in North Street. It was at this time that a new enlarged entrance was made from Market Street to allow Robinson's large four-horse vans to enter the premises. The properties were eventually sub-divided into two separate premises and by 1834 Mr. Summerton Bennett, the new owner of the Steyne Hotel had, in the face of considerable opposition from the owners of the houses in the Steyne, purchased 'Paines field' and constructed new stables and a coach house at the rear of his hotel. The central entrance from Ann Street was then blocked off and the premises were divided east to west and a new entrance was provided to the right of the old one. Richard Robinson moved his entire operation from Market Street to the western end of the Ann Street premises and a forge was erected on the eastern side. In 1871 the western portion of the stables was purchased by Mr Edward Snewin, who then demolished them and constructed six houses on the site known as Sussex Place, later numbered 21–31 Ann Street.[146]

Although Edward Ogle had, by 1808, sold most of the western end of 'Mole Soals' as building plots he had retained all the land to the east of the theatre as a kitchen garden.[147] However, on the 2nd October 1808 he sold the south eastern corner to Mr. John Shearsmith, a surgeon, for £230.0s.0d. The substantial house built on this plot of land (originally No. 4 High street, but later No. 9) had two entrances in Ann Street, one of which was the entrance to his surgery. Edward Snewin suggests that although Dr. Shearsmith was a very clever doctor he was not very successful when handling his finances,[148] and it may well be for this reason that he sold his house just over a year later to James Penfold, a yeoman of Goring. It does, however, appear that Dr. Shearsmith continued to live in the property. James Penfold was, unfortunately, equally unsuccessful in handling his financial affairs, for by 1819 he was bankrupt. Of necessity he sold this property to Henry Budd Esq., who one month later sold it to Mr. Joseph Dickenson Croskey of London who still owned the property during the 1820's.

On the 20th July 1810, James Penfold had also acquired from Edward Ogle for £296.0s.0d. the part of 'Mole Soals' that was immediately to the north of Dr. Shearsmith's house and it would appear from the wording on the deed that James Penfold had already started constructing a house on it prior to the purchase. Two years later, on the 9th July 1812, James Penfold sold the property to John Nickles, who still resided in the property in 1821.[149] It would appear that Edward Ogle had, by c. 1810, also sold the remaining part of the eastern end of 'mole soals' to a James Johnson.[150] This plot immediately to the north of John Nickle's house (formerly No. 5, later No. 11 High Street), shown as vacant land on Phillips' map 1814, was sold by James Johnson to John Nickles, who, by 1821 had erected two houses on it. The northern of these two houses was conveyed to William Prescott, a corn merchant, on 24th January 1821. The southern of the two houses was also conveyed to William Prescott on 4th May 1825 and the combined property was subsequently known as Palmerston House.

By the February of 1809, not quite six years after the passing of the Worthing Town Act, the Board of Town Commissioners was already in financial difficulties. The town had expanded so rapidly that the sum of money that they were empowered to borrow on the credit of the rate assessments had become totally inadequate to light, pave, drain and police the town. Because of this, and other matters in the initial Act that required either ramification or modification, the Town Commissioners made application to Parliament to amend and enlarge their powers. In addition they also sought authorisation to construct a Market House[151]

> 'for in their opinion it would be a great Advantage and Accommodation to the Inhabitants of the said Town of Worthing, and of all Persons resorting thereto, if a Market for all kinds of Meat, Fish, Poultry, Butter and Garden Stuff were established within the said town.'[152]

Parliament acquiesced to the Town Commissioners' requests and the necessary act was passed by them in month of July 1809. This amending Act empowered the Town Commissioners to set up a market and increased their borrowing limit from £2,000 to £5,000 with the ability to borrow another £4,000 on the security of the market tolls.[153]

The Town Commissioners wasted very little time, for on the 7th July 1809 they instructed the Clerk to seek tenders for the purchase of a piece of ground in the town of Worthing, not less than 100 feet [30.48 metres] in width and 150 feet [45.72 metres] in length, for the purpose of erecting a Market House. They further stipulated that, as required by the Act, the said land should have proper roads leading to it.[154] One month later, at a meeting held on 1st August 1809, at the insistence of Edward Ogle the Town Commissioners agreed to purchase a piece of land in Ann Street[155] for the sum of £1050-0s-0d. from James Hopkins (banker) on which to build the new Market House.[156] The composite land parcel in question was, however, not legally his to sell. The southern portion was part of 'Mole Soals', still in the ownership of Edward Ogle, and the northern portion was part of 'Longs Garden', still in the ownership of Richard Cook. It would appear that while still wishing to influence and possibly gain financially from the chosen location for the Market House neither Edward Ogle or Richard Cook were prepared to give up their position as Town Commissioners, for included in the amending parliamentary Act of 1809 was a requirement that no Town Commissioner should materially benefit, either directly or indirectly from any contract or work to be executed under the powers of the Act or enjoy any beneficial employment.[157]

Edward Ogle made good the situation in respect of his land very rapidly, for on the 8th August 1809 he sold his portion of the land to James Hopkins for £514-10s-0d. Richard Cook was far more dilatory for he did not sell his portion of 'Longs Garden' to James Hopkins (for £294.0s.0d.) until the 1st February 1810. The Town Commissioners were not, however, conveyed the overall land parcel, which only measured 70 feet [21.34 metres] wide by 144 feet [43.89 metres] long, until the 10th August 1810, some six weeks after the official opening of the market. One can only assume that James Hopkins was not too concerned, for having sold the overall land parcel to the Commissioners for £1050-0s-0d it would appear he made £247-10s-0d. on the overall transaction.[158]

Although the legalities for the transfer of the land took nearly a year it did not stop the Town Commissioners implementing the design and construction of the Market House. Having agreed to purchase the land from James Hopkins at the beginning of August 1809, at their meeting on the 11th September[159] they ratified the status of both Ann Street and Brook Street as Public Highways to satisfy the requirement in the Act that the Market House should have proper roads leading to it. A month later Edward Hide, who was also the architect responsible for the theatre, was appointed to prepare plans and elevations of the building.[160] His accepted design was for a rectangular building which extended from Ann Street to Market Street. Inside there were covered stalls on all four sides, the roof being supported internally on columns, around a quadrangle with a pump in the centre. The elevation facing Market Street was to be constructed in red brick and the Ann Street elevation in white brick. In each of these elevations he proposed imposing gateways with iron gates.[161]

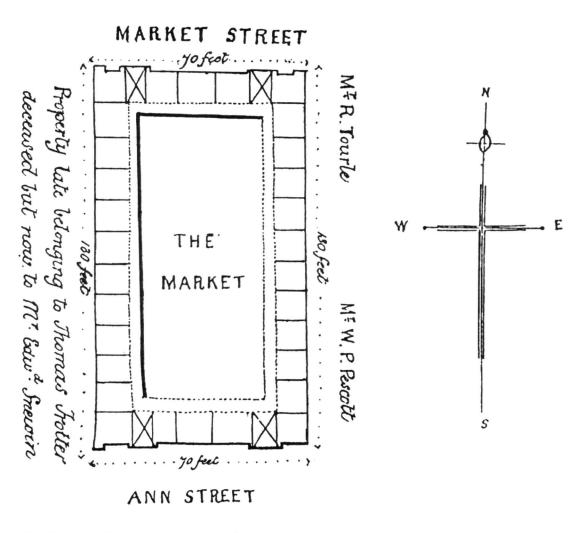

Fig. 72 *Plan of the Market House, Ann Street*

Construction commenced in the March of 1810.[162] The bricklaying was carried out by Richard Cook, who had sold the northern portion of the land to the Commissioners; the carpentry work by John & Edward Hide; the plumbing work by Richard Palmer, whose house and workshop was opposite the site, on the southern side of Ann Street; the iron work by Mr George White, whose workshop was in North Street; and the stonework by John Joanes, whose yard also fronted Ann Street, being located behind his house in Warwick Street. As a condition of undertaking their works all these tradesmen accepted a security on the market tolls as payment for their endeavours ![163]

By the June of 1810 the construction of the Market House (marked 70 on Fig.49) was complete and the Town Commissioners placed a notice in the *Sussex Weekly Journal* stating the Market would be opened on Monday the 2nd July 1810 and the stalls, sheds, etc. would be let at their next meeting.[164] The allocation of the stalls was determined by a ballot at a meeting held at the Nelson Inn at the end of June presided over by the Market Committee, which comprised Edward Ogle, Michael Morrah and James Hopkins. At the same meeting the rent for each stall was set at £12-12s-0d. per year. [165]

Fig. 73 *The old Market entrance*

The Market opened on the 2nd July 1810. The three stalls occupied by the fishmongers were located on the south side of the Market House. Two were used by Messrs. Davis and Primmer and one by Mr. Cook. Their stalls were lead covered slabs with a drain to allow the water to drain off. The butchers, many of whom came from Thakeham and West Chiltington, were located on the west side. The greengrocers and fruiterers were located on the east side, and the poulterers (who came from Findon, Bramber and adjacent villages) were located on the north side. The space in the centre of the Market was divided down the middle by a narrow paving-stone about five inches wide, and it was on this that china and crockery dealers used to display their wares. Outside were wattle enclosures for pigs and other livestock.[166] The Market was open between 7am and 4pm from May to November and between 8am and 2pm from December to April.[167] Saturday was the principal market day, when the farmers from the neighbouring villages brought their produce to the town in carts and wagons. Every morning about nine o'clock the fish, poultry and vegetables on sale that day were cried throughout the town by the Town Crier. To signify the opening and closing of the Market a bell was rung. A specific bell for this purpose was not, however, purchased by the Treasurer of the Market until the June of 1817.[168] Why the Market Bell illustrated on page 106 of *The Worthing Map Story* is dated 1806 remains a mystery !

On the 9th July 1810 Mr John Butcher was appointed, at a yearly salary of £52.10s.0d., as the Clerk of the Market to receive the market tolls.[169] Prior to the opening of the Market Mr. Richard Palmer was employed to paint the table of tolls that was displayed in the Market House and a hand bill disclosing these tolls was circulated throughout the town.[170] The level of tolls charged at Worthing Market was as follows:

'Butchers were charged 1s.0d.per day, as was any other stall holder selling items not included in the table of tolls. A fisherman selling his own fish had to pay 4d. a basket if it contained 2 gallons or less, 8d. if it contained half a bushel or less and 3s.6d if it was more than a bushel. For every gallon of cockles or mussels the toll was 1d. and on 100 shrimps 1/2d. For a live pig only 2d. was taken, but for a dead pig 4d. was charged. On a turkey or goose, the toll was 2d., on six chickens, ducks or rabbits 3d., with a lower scale for a larger number up to 1s.3d. for four dozen of each. For twelve pounds of butter a toll of 3d. was paid, and for two dozen eggs 2d. Vegetables were charged at 2d. up to 1/2 bushel, and 3d. a bushel.'[171]

Following its opening in 1810, the Market was financially successful for a number of years as there were relatively few shops or business houses in the town in direct competition. With efficient management it could easily have been made into a popular and successful institution, but due to its complete mismanagement it quickly started to become a drain on the town's limited revenue. The Town Commissioners were regularly receiving complaints regarding the methods of certain local market traders. It would appear that due to a sheer lack of control these traders had been able to monopolise the market by actively preventing traders from other parts of the county attending the market, by buying up their competitor's merchandise, and in some instances re-selling the produce purchased at enhanced prices. As a consequence, in 1816 the Town Commissioners took the Market 'back into their own hands', and revised the Market Regulations prohibiting 'Forestalling, Engrossing and Regrating' in an attempt to overcome these unacceptable trading practices. To reinforce their resolve they also limited each trader to one stall, imposing a fine of 20 shillings (£1.00) for each infringement of this rule and offering a reward of £5.0s.0d to any person giving information about anyone breaking the new regulations. The Town Commissioners also produced bills, which were distributed throughout the town, and placed an advert in the *Lewes Journal* stating they were 'determined to stop what had been practised, [and] hereby give notice that they will [now] encourage every County Dealer [to attend the market on a regular basis].'[172]

Having tried to regularise the method of trading in the Market, the Town Commissioners, in the hope of increasing revenue, very unwisely had the numbers on the stalls painted out, (it is said) during the night, and had them re-numbered, so that the stall previously numbered 1 was now 1 and 2 - thus making the stall-holders pay a double toll or share per stall. As a result of this sharp practice many of the better-class stall holders were driven out and took shops in the town, and the reputation of the Market further declined.[173] By 1859 the Market was dilapidated and was sold to Edward Snewin,[174] whose building company used it as a builder's yard until it was demolished in 1969 to make way for the Guildbourne Centre.

Many fashionable people had stayed at Worthing during the first decade of the nineteenth century and *The Times* of the 28th September 1811 records the resort as being crowded with fashionable visitors during both August and September. Although nearby Brighton attracted a larger number of visitors it had a reputation for noise and disruption which rendered it unpopular with certain sections of society and this helped to enhance Worthing's reputation as a select resort.[175] The resort function was now beginning to dominate Worthing's economy and additional land was needed for both housing and commercial premises for the increasing residential and seasonal population. Apart from the area around Warwick Street, which was quite densely developed, most of the initial expansion of the town had taken place on old enclosed parcels of land that lay on either side of Cross Lane (today Montague Street) and the southern end of the route of Old Worthing Street and because of the fragmented ownership of these land parcels development had, of necessity, been both small and piecemeal.

The large medieval open fields still remained untouched and it would appear that the consensus in favour of enclosing them was prompted by the expectation that the larger allotted parcels of land would more readily allow further building development, rather than by a desire to improve agricultural techniques and production. Although the Worthing Inclosure Act was passed in 1805[177] the resultant redistribution of land was not fully implemented until 1810, when it brought to an end the 'custom and practice' of open or common field cultivation that had continued unhindered from at least the medieval period. It completely altered the topography, for the land in the former 347 acres [140.4 hectares] of the common fields was re-distributed into large rectangular fields, each allotment being equal to the combined area of each owner's previously held strips in the open fields. As will be seen, for those recipients whose awards were located close to the already established town, this redistribution of land proved to be, in the long term, very advantageous.

By 1810 only twenty-six people held land in the open fields. Nearly all held consolidated 'multiple estates' which successive owners had engrossed or acquired either by inheritance or purchase. The gradual penetration of capitalism during the seventeenth and eighteenth centuries had provided the motivation for the expansion of both cereal and sheep farming on the coastal plain of Sussex. Profits from the sale of surplus grain and sheep at the local, regional and London markets had provided the means for the tenants of the larger holdings to engross or acquire the adjacent or nearby land of the smaller 'subsistence' land holders in the common fields to create more compact and more manageable blocks of land.[178] Most of the early sixteenth-century landholdings had been small 'subsistence' farms, and in many cases their associated dwellings or farmhouses had been built on the crofts and closes that adjoined either side of Worthing Street. Although the names of many of these former subsistence landholdings are recorded in the surviving manorial documents, in a large number of cases the location of both the land and associated dwellings have faded into obscurity. As has been seen earlier (in Chapter 3) several of these early farmhouses did survive and this is why certain of the nineteenth-century multiple estates often contained more than one dwelling or farmhouse. In many cases the owners of the late eighteenth- and early nineteenth-century estates were absentee landlords who let both their land and surviving farmhouses to tenants whose names are often identified with the individual farms.

By circa 1814 the initial development boom was over and there were many empty houses and surplus accommodation.[179] The resort, however, continued to develop, albeit at a slower rate,[180] and the earliest street plan of Worthing produced by H. Phillips, published in 1814 in the second edition of John Evans' *Picture of Worthing*, shows the town at the end of its rapid initial growth into a 'fashionable Georgian watering place'.

Adjacent to the foreshore were buildings extending from Warwick Buildings in the east to Prospect Place in the west. The sixteen lodging houses known as Warwick Buildings (marked 71 on Fig. 75) were constructed after 1809 on the old enclosure known as 'Long Croft' following its sub-division into building plots by its owner Richard Stubbs. A deed

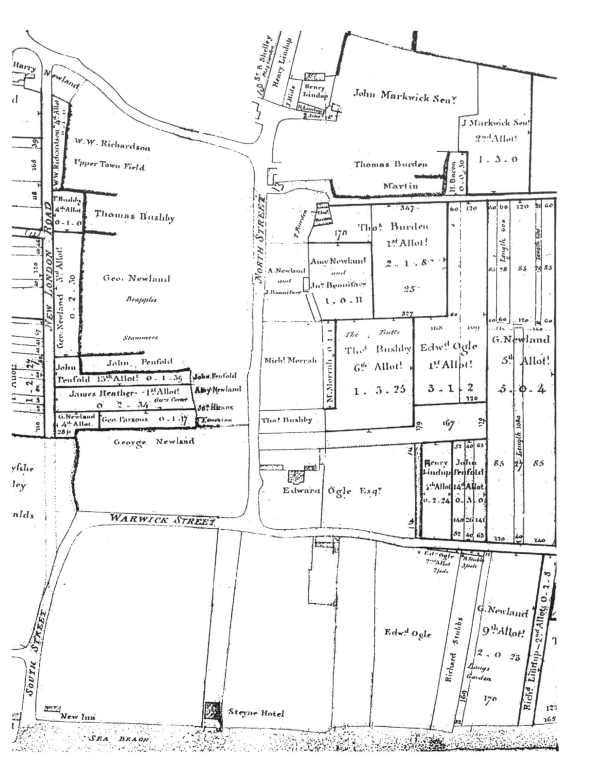

Fig. 74 *Extract of plan for Worthing Inclosure award* [176]

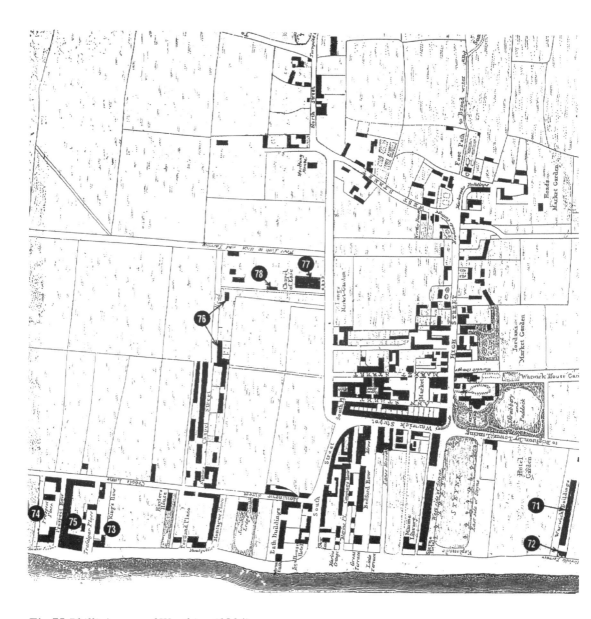

Fig.75 *Phillip's map of Worthing (1814)*

reveals that the southernmost of these building plots, on which Greville or Gravel Terrace (marked 72 on Fig. 75) was subsequently erected, was sold in 1809 to Richard Palmer, plumber, for £250.0s.0d.[181]

Those residing in Warwick Buildings had an unrestricted view of Steyne Gardens. Worthing's original promenade had been its sands, but by 1811 they had been replaced by the Steyne,[182] which had been modelled on the recreational area of the same name at Brighton. In the summer of 1812 a local band was formed which started to perform in Steyne Gardens in the evening but, according to Henfrey Smail,

> 'the musicians were more enthusiastic than skilful and after the neighbourhood had
> put up with their doleful wailings for several evenings they were by unanimous
> demand disbanded.'[183]

Regimental bands stationed in the area during the Napoleonic Wars had regularly performed in the town[184] and the band of the Worthing contingent of the South Bramber Volunteers offered its services: they proved to be a great improvement on the local band and quickly became an attraction for the town's visitors.

By 1821 the Steyne had been superseded by the Esplanade, which immediately became the fashionable place for the visitors to rendezvous - to promenade remained an essential part of the resort routine. As Phillips' map clearly shows, prior to its construction there was only a rough narrow road between the beach and the properties that immediately adjoined the foreshore. There were no sea defences, and during the winter gales the sea often came over the road and flooded the lawns towards Montague Street. The Esplanade, which was constructed from Greville Terrace to West Buildings, was looked upon as a great improvement to the town,[185] and was the closest a visitor could get to the sea until piers were constructed in the Victorian period. According to Wallis' Guide of 1826,

> 'This delightful walk was formed in the year 1821, and it is a great improvement to the town, being always dry and clean, and well lighted by night by a row of handsome lamps. The promenade extends along the beach from Gravel Terrace to West Terrace, having the carriage road between it and the houses. It is twenty feet wide and above half a mile in length. Nothing can excel the spectacle which it presents when thronged (as it is every fine summer's evening) with all the beauty and fashion of the place; while the opportunity it presents for inhaling the ocean breeze in unalloyed purity, and the defence it affords against the sea, stamp it with an importance commensurate with its attractive appearance.'[186]

Fig. 76 *First aerial perspective of the town of Worthing showing Warwick Buildings on left*

At the western end of the town, Kings Row (marked 73 on Fig. 75) and Prospect Place (marked 74 on Fig. 75), a pleasant row of small houses that overlooked a lawn, had been constructed adjacent to the foreshore by 1807.[187] According to *Mackoull's Guide* of 1811, the first four houses in Trafalgar Place (marked 75 on Fig. 75) were built and furnished as lodging houses by a Mr. France, an upholsterer of Pall Mall.[188] Trafalgar Place was renamed Augusta Place, after Princess Augusta stayed at Trafalgar House whilst visiting Worthing in 1829. It became the Stanhoe Hotel in *c*.1900, which was demolished in 1948 and is now the site of the modern Augusta House.[189]

The provision of cheaper housing was essential if the town was to continue to expand, for it was needed to house the less affluent tradesmen, servants and the poor. Terraces of cheaper houses had been constructed, infilling the vacant plots. Financed by local builders and tradesmen these were, ironically, very profitable and far less speculative than providing either resort amenities or accommodation for visitors to the town. To the north of Montague Street and to the east and west of High Street the land remained primarily agricultural as few of the post-enclosure rectangular fields had, as yet, been built on. Houses had, however, been constructed in Belle Vue (marked 76 on Fig. 75) on land that had previously been part of the former West field.

A Chapel of Ease, had also been erected (marked 77 on Fig. 75) on a plot of land 73 feet [22.25 metres] wide and 133 feet [40.54 metres] deep at the eastern end of the '2nd Allotment' of land awarded to George Newland under the Inclosure Act.[190] The building, designed by J. B. Rebecca,[191] was consecrated in 1812[192] but remained a Chapel of Ease until 1894. The chapel was built by subscriptions, and money to maintain it and pay the incumbent was raised by the sale or leasing of pews and by a rate levied on the pews' proprietors. Most of the proprietors were those who let the lodgings and furnished houses.[193] The first houses in Ambrose Place (marked 78 on Fig. 75) named after Ambrose Cartwright, had also been built on George Newland's 'allotted' land and stood alongside the Chapel of Ease in splendid isolation on the western side of Chapel Road.

Chapel Road, named after the Chapel of Ease, was laid out as part of the enclosure process to bypass High Street, which it had replaced as the main entrance to the town by 1817.[194] The improvement in road access, brought about by the opening of the new turnpike road in 1804, had encouraged the Town Commissioners to plan a new road from the Teville Gate to the top of South Street 'to give Worthing a more impressive entrance'.[195] Although the northern section had been constructed by 1812, providing access to both the Chapel of Ease and Ambrose Place, it is surprising that the road is shown as being complete for its entire length on Phillips' map of 1814, for it was not until the March of 1815 that the 'Town Commissioners first applied to Sir Timothy Shelley, Baronet, for permission to extend the road through the 'Wales field' owned by him.[196] For some unknown reason in the minutes of the Town Commissioners meetings the name of the ancient enclosure known as the 'Wealds', (first recorded on the Broadwater manorial survey of 1300), is occasionally corrupted to 'Whales' or 'Wales'.[197] Pre-empting Sir Timothy Shelley's reply, the Town Commissioners instructed their surveyor to produce a plan and mark the proposed line of the outstanding length of road from the Chapel of Ease to South Street.[198] At their meeting held on the 20th August 1815 the Town Commissioners thanked Sir Timothy Shelley,

> 'for the handsome manner in which he has assisted the Commissioners in obtaining
> a new road through the "Wales field" into South Street.'[199]

These thanks were possibly a little premature, for the construction of this length of road was not finally authorised by them until the 19th December 1815, some four months later,

Fig. 77 *Chapel of Ease and Ambrose Place*

following a protracted exchange of correspondence between their solicitors and the solicitors acting on behalf of the trustees of the late Sir Bysshe Shelley.[200] Unfortunately, even then, the complex legal arrangements were not totally resolved, for the Town Commissioners were still having difficulties in completing both the contract of the sale with the solicitors of the late Sir Bysshe Shelley and the enfranchisement of the road by the lord of the Manor of Broadwater, who still held the manorial rights to the land on which the road had been constructed. Due to these problems Chapel Road, from the Chapel of Ease to its junction with South Street, was not declared a Public Highway until the 23rd March 1816, when it was advertised as such in the *Sussex Weekly Journal*, in accordance with the procedure for the declaration of Public Highways laid out in the Town Act of 1803.[201] When Chapel Road was finally opened in 1816 it rapidly displaced the centuries-old narrow circuitous route to the sea via High Street, and the former cottages and farmsteads of the ancient hamlet that had remained a distinct cluster to the north of the emerging town gradually became engulfed as it slowly expanded northwards.

During the early 1820's the town was still being frequented by fashionable visitors[202] and by 1822 the town was also attracting winter visitors.[203] In dramatic contrast to the two shopkeepers, a carpenter and a bricklayer recorded in 1798[204] there were over thirty shopkeepers by 1820 dealing in food and confectionery as well as clothiers, jewellers, perfumers, booksellers and stationers. There were also coachmakers and over a dozen people connected with the expanding building industry.[205]

Development continued, albeit much more slowly than during the first two decades of the nineteenth century. Beach House, with its stable, coach houses and grounds that stretched down to the sea, had for many years formed a barrier to the town's continued eastward development. It was constructed by 1820 for Robert Elwes from designs by the local architect John Rebecca. This three-storey building, with a brick and rendered exterior, which still exists today, has been described as being 'Worthing's most stately and dignified Georgian Mansion'.[206]

To the east of the Steyne Warwick Place, north of the lower Brighton Road, had been laid out by 1826 and Alfred Place was built between 1826 and 1843.[207] Union Place had also been laid out by 1826 to link Chapel Road and High Street. New houses and terraces had also been built to the south of Montague Street and by 1826 the built-up area of the town had reached West Buildings. At the western end of the town West Street and Surrey Street consisted of smaller houses inhabited by fishermen,[208] and this area became inhabited by a disproportionate number of Worthing's poorer residents by the end of the Georgian period.[209]

Life for the poor in the early years of the nineteenth century was very different to today. There was no welfare state and many died at a very early age due to the lack of basic medical care. Their plight did not go unnoticed, for at a public meeting held on the 20th August 1820, chaired by the Rev. Henry Dixon, it was unanimously resolved

> 'That a dispensary for administering medicines and medical advice gratis for the relief of the sick and necessitous poor would be a great advantage and utility to the town of Worthing and the neighbourhood. That such an establishment be accordingly instituted in Ann Street, Worthing, under the name of "Worthing Dispensary". That the Dispensary be open daily, except Sundays, from 10 till 11 in the forenoon, and in the case of accidents, attention to be given at all times by the medical officer of the establishment on the recommendation of one of the governors.'[210]

This Dispensary, which used two of the ground floor rooms of the house immediately adjoining the western side of the theatre in Ann Street, was opened only two days later at 10am on the 31st August 1829. Its first physician was I.G. Cloves; Frederick Dixon was the consulting surgeon and William Munday Jnr. dispensed the medicines prescribed by them. By the end of 1829, over five hundred patients had been treated, supported by contributions received from both inhabitants and visitors.

Unfortunately, as was frequently the case with voluntary hospitals, the funds of the Dispensary were sound found to be insufficient for its needs. Funds were so low by 1833 that a Grand Bazaar was held under the patronage of Her Royal Highness the Princess Augusta at Parson's Assembly Rooms (part of the Steyne Hotel). Within a few years another Bazaar had to be held to raise further funds to enable the Dispensary to continue.[211] By 1844 this building was considered to be inadequate and in 1846 the Dispensary was moved to a purpose-built building at the western end of Ann Street.

Prior to 1820 the expansion of the town had been piecemeal, constrained by both the size and orientation of the ancient enclosed land parcels on which the town's initial development had taken place. There had been no grandiose schemes comparable in either size or style with the squares and crescents that had been erected at Hove, Brighton and Kemp Town. Although Worthing's continued development was now much slower, larger and more stylish buildings were now being erected to attract those upper and middle class visitors who still chose to visit the English seaside.

York Terrace, originally a terrace of five separate lodging houses, was erected in c. 1822 by Edward Evershed on 'Low Field' immediately to the east of the Steyne, and its stucco facade, ionic pilasters, porches and balconies created one of Worthing's most impressive Regency frontages. The complete terrace later became Warnes Hotel, which burned down in 1987.[212]

Fig. 78 Beach House

Fig. 79 Ann Street Dispensary (1829)

Fig. 80 *York Terrace*

In 1826, two years after Oliver Hillman took over the ownership of the New Inn, facing the sea on the south-eastern corner of South Street, its name was changed to the Marine Hotel. It was probably rebuilt or enlarged with the pleasant bow-fronted Regency appearance shown in the figure below.[213]

Fig. 81 *Marine Hotel (1849)*

In 1824, the old eighteenth-century Sea House Inn on the south-western corner of South Street was demolished. It was replaced by the Sea House Hotel, a Regency-style building

SEA HOUSE HOTEL,
Worthing, October, 21ˢᵗ, 1826.

Sir,
       I beg to inform you, that the OPENING DINNER *of the* NEW SEA HOUSE HOTEL, *is fixed for* MONDAY, the 30ᵗʰ, Instant, *when the honor of your Company, and that of your Friends, will much oblige.*

Sir,
Your obedient humble Servant,

G. PARSONS.

———————————

An application for Tickets before Saturday, will be esteemed a favour.

———————————

Tickets 15s. including a Bottle of Wine and Desert.

———————————

DINNER ON TABLE AT FIVE O'CLOCK.

Fig. 82 Sea House Hotel

designed by John Rebecca, which became Worthing's largest and finest hotel until it was destroyed by fire on the 21st May 1901. The Worthing Arcade now occupies the site.[214]

Situated immediately to the north of Montague Street was Liverpool Terrace with its imposing line of bow fronts, designed by Henry Cotton and named after the Earl of Liverpool (R.B.Jenkins, who was Prime Minister between 1826 and 1827). It had been built speculatively by John James between 1826 and 1833 on the former enclosed parcel of land called 'London Fields'.[215] Although initially only the southern six houses of this terrace were constructed on the embanked site, according to Edward Snewin, these 'houses let well and six more were then built on a slightly different plan, having a balcony in front supported by pillars'. There was a gated entrance from Montague Street marked by four tall piers. The houses in this terrace faced towards Chapel Road across what remained open 'pleasure grounds' until *c.* 1870.[216]

Fig. 83 Liverpool Terrace

Park Crescent, the most imposing and impressive piece of architecture of the period at Worthing, planned and designed by Amon Wilds, the Regency architect of Brighton, was also built between 1826 and 1833. It lay detached from the town on the crest of a ridge close to the Heene boundary.[217] When conceived it combined terraced with detached housing, a south-facing crescent, serpentine in plan, ornamental grounds containing a pair of 'cottage ornees' and a massive gateway with herms fronting Richmond Road. The scheme was, however, never completed due to lack of capital. Only the 'cottage ornees' and the crescent of thirteen houses and lodge gate with its giant pilasters of unusual design were erected, by a Brighton builder named Sawyer.[218] A second entrance in Wykeham Road, similar to the one in Richmond Road, and four villas, two detached and a semi-detached pair in a similar style to the crescent, were never completed.[219] The completed Gothic style 'Swiss Cottages' became the 'Beechwood Hall Hotel' in 1933.[220]

Fig.84 Park Crescent

Worthing is described in Wallis's guide book of 1826 as 'select and particularly suitable for children on account of its quietness, decorum, and safe sea bathing'.[221] Its reputation for quietness may, however, been partly caused by the economic depression which was beginning to effect it from the mid 1820's. The first quarter of the nineteenth century has been described as the 'The Golden Age of Worthing'.[222] The emerging town had catered exclusively for a limited number of visitors drawn from the wealthy and fashionable classes, who had travelled to the town by either coach or post chaise, stayed at the most expensive lodging houses and patronised the warm baths, libraries and the theatre. The local tradesmen together with the former fishing and agricultural community had become almost entirely dependent on the visitors who brought wealth into the town, that was quite disproportionate to their numbers. Investment in the emerging Georgian seaside resorts was, however, far less stable than agriculture, commerce or transport because it was totally dependent upon the marginal disposable income of the small upper, middle and landed classes in Britain and, more importantly, on sustaining their interest in the seaside.[223] In the years of peace that followed the Napoleonic Wars the 'fashionable' again went abroad for their recreation. All the emerging seaside resorts in Sussex were suffering competition from resorts elsewhere in Britain and as the depression became more general throughout the country most lost even more of their established clientele. In the autumn of 1826 many of the county banks failed and people no longer had as much money as before to spend on amusement.[224] The late eighteenth- and early nineteenth-century mode of holiday, with its 'select company', libraries and assemblies suddenly collapsed.[225]

In the first twenty-five years of the nineteenth century the town of Worthing had expanded far beyond the capacity of its rateable value and the Town Commissioners had neither the powers nor the ability to deal with the situation. From as early as 1818 it was clearly apparent that the expenditure of Worthing's Town Commissioners was exceeding their sources of revenue, and a committee was appointed to ascertain both the extent of the deficiency and to consider what measures might be incorporated in a further Act of Parliament to remedy the situation.[226] The committee found a very unsatisfactory financial situation. In addition to many unpaid bills, three years' interest on the loan raised by the Town Commissioners on the security of the town's rates remained outstanding. Their detailed scrutiny of the Town Commissioners' accounts also revealed the revenue from the town's market had been so deficient that two and a half years' interest remained outstanding on the loan of £4,000 obtained for its construction,[227] raised on the security of the revenue from the market tolls.[228]

At a special meeting called by the Town Commissioners on the 17th November 1820 it was resolved that 'the consideration of obtaining a new Act of Parliament, first raised on the 24th July 1818, be revived, for all those present considered it would be "expedient" to obtain a new Act of Parliament "for the benefit of the town"'.[229] The new Act was passed in 1821 and raised the paving rate from 2s-6d [12.5p] in the pound to 3s-6d [17.5p] in the pound, and increased the Town Commissioners' borrowing limit on the security of the market by a further £1,200. This new Act also regulated the construction of new buildings and extended the Town Commissioners' powers to include provisions for the licensing of hackney coaches, sedan chairs and bathing machines and the regulation of bathing, boats and huts on the beach.[230]

The Town Commissioners were also empowered to charge a duty on coal brought into the town, on the security of which they were able to borrow another £3,000. Henry Partington Esq., the Collector of the Customs at Shoreham, was appointed as the 'Collector of the Duties' payable for coals, calm, coke, cinders and charcoal brought by vessels to the town. Thomas Trotter was authorised by the Town Commissioners to collect the duties, on behalf of Henry Partington, at a salary not exceeding ten pounds per annum. John Hickox was appointed as one of the 'Land Coal meters, and the sealer and maker of sacks and measures used in the coal trade'. It was further authorised that the place for sealing and making the sacks would be John Hickox' house in High Street, and that the seal and mark would be 'Neptunes Trident'.[231]

The coal came by sea and was brought to the town in small Newcastle collier brigs, called 'Geordies'. Being flat-bottomed, the sturdy little vessels were run ashore at high tide and the coal was unloaded using horses and carts.[232] John Evans describes the slow but picturesque process in the town's first guide book:

Several of these vessels in the summer are to be seen left by the tide on the beach, their appearance from the keel upwards to the extremity of the masts produces novel impressions at a place where nothing but small fishing boats meet the eye in every direction…. The coal is unladen and conveyed into the village by an awkward and tedious operation, for it might be much better accomplished. A gentleman skilled in navel architecture, who visited Worthing, showed me an ingenious plan, which he had drawn up for the purpose, well entitled to attention.'[233]

Despite the provisions of the 1821 Act the Town Commissioners' financial position never improved. The successive raising of the limit of their borrowing was symptomatic of their financial difficulties, which were again exacerbated by a further decline in the revenue from the market. As each year passed more and more stall-holders had left the market to establish shops of their own in the expanding town. As a consequence it became increasingly difficult to find a bidder for the market tolls, which were auctioned each year in June, and in 1825 the Town Commissioners were forced to take the total management of the market into their own hands. The Market House was put into good repair and James Bassett was appointed as 'Collector of the Market Tolls' at a salary of £25.0s.0d per annum.[234] Unfortunately this did little to help the situation and the Town Commissioners became increasingly ineffective in dealing with the town's problems as more and more of their income from the paving rate and market tolls was, of necessity, used to pay off the interest charges on the various loans.

By 1829 the Town Commissioners were facing a major financial crisis. The town was on the verge of bankruptcy. Business was at a standstill, hotels and lodging houses were empty, the town's debts and official salaries remained unpaid and a number of the local officials were dismissed, their duties being temporarily undertaken by unpaid volunteers.[235] The situation had been accentuated by the outdated and haphazard approach to the rate assessments that had evolved and the anomaly that Broadwater and Worthing were still treated as a single unit for rating purposes, the smaller but rapidly expanding town having to bear a disproportionate share of the expenses. This was not a situation unique to Worthing, for a similar state of affairs was to be found in other rapidly growing urban centres throughout the country; it was to remedy such anomalies that the Parochial Assessment Act had been passed by Parliament in 1837.

At a public meeting held at the Boys' National School on the 18th August 1837, it was decided that in the light of the financial difficulties being experienced it was appropriate that a map and valuation be prepared of all the land, houses and other buildings in the Parish of Broadwater in order that a new and equitable assessment could be made in conformity with the Parochial Assessment Act.[236] Mr. Charles Hide's tender of 95 guineas for a survey and map and Mr. James Penfold's tender of £95 for a valuation were accepted in December 1837 by the Assessment Committee appointed at the public meeting.[237]

Never before had such a comprehensive survey been attempted at Worthing and considering the extensive area it covered it is not surprising that Charles Hide did not complete his map until the 1st June 1838, some four months after the agreed date. Drawn to a scale of 25 inches to a mile, Charles Hide's map covers the entire Parish of Broadwater, of which Worthing was still a part, from the boundary with Heene to Lancing and as far north as Cissbury Ring. The original, and only known, copy, which is now lodged at the West Sussex Record Office at Chichester, measures 8.5 feet [2.6 metres] by 5.5 feet [1.68 metres] and is coloured and mounted on rollers. Each individual plot of land is numbered and cross-referenced to a separate schedule, which although thought lost has been recently re-discovered by the authors. This is also now deposited at the West Sussex Record Office.

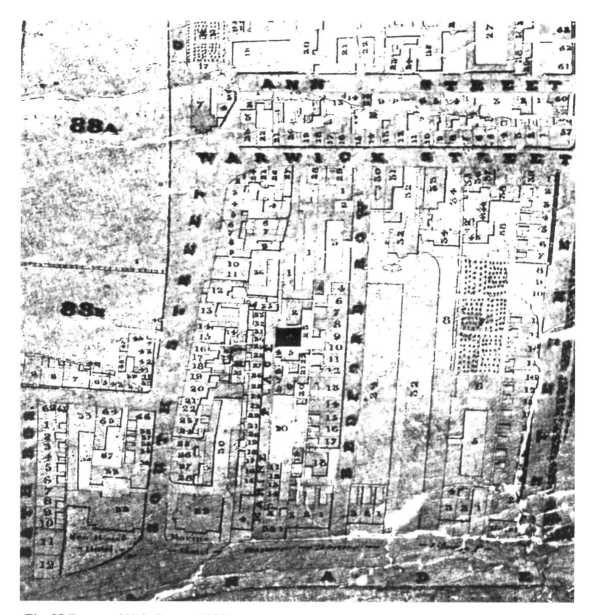

Fig. 85 Extract of Hide Survey (1838)

Being prepared at the beginning of the Victorian period to an accurate scale, its content is not only of interest but important for it records, in detail, the development of the town and the end of its evolution into a seaside resort.

For the first thirty-two years of its existence as a town Worthing did not have a Town Hall and the Town Commissioners held their meetings at the Nelson Inn in South Street from the 13th June 1803 until the 14th February 1812 when they changed their venue to the Royal George in Market Street.[238] On several occasions, at the meetings of the Town Commissioners, the possibility of supplying a public clock and the building of a Town Hall was raised[239] and in response to an eloquent address in 1818 by Dr. Michael Morrah, the local surgeon, sufficient monies were collected not only to erect a turret clock, but also to

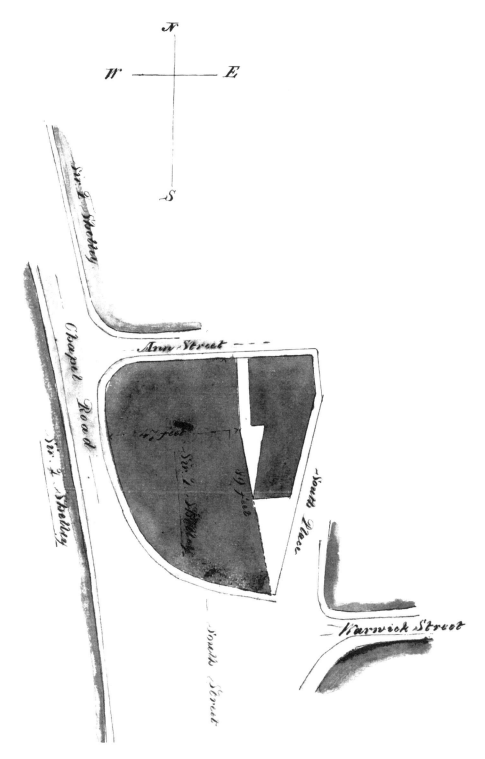

Fig. 86 Plan of the old Town Hall site

build a Town Hall beneath it.[240] In the knowledge that funds were available, the 1821 Act of Parliament which widened the Town Commissioners' powers to make improvements to the town also included a clause that stating

> 'that it shall and may be lawful to and for the said Commissioners, whenever they deem it necessary and expedient to purchase a Town Clock, and keep the same in good repair, and to erect and put up the clock in such part of the said Town as they shall think proper: Provided always, that the expense of purchasing and putting up such clock shall not exceed the sum of Two hundred Pounds.'[241]

The same Act also allowed the Town Commissioners to purchase any piece of land in the town for erecting on it any building or room for the purpose of holding their meetings, provided that the cost of the land did not exceed five hundred pounds and the cost of the building did not exceed one thousand pounds.

In January 1825 Mr. Harry Newland and the Clerk to the Town Commissioners were authorised to negotiate with Sir Timothy Shelley for the purchase of the isolated part of the 'Wealds', bounded by Ann Street, South Place, Chapel Road and South Street on which to build a Town Hall.[242] It has been stated that the negotiations resulted in Sir Timothy Shelley giving the land as a gift to the town. The official documents held in Worthing Borough Council's archive, however, clearly show this was not the case. On the 10th March 1834 William Tribe, the clerk to the Town Commissioners, wrote to Sir Timothy Shelley on their behalf, informing him of their desire to purchase his land 'for the purpose of erecting a building (called a Town Hall)'. In the letter he also advised Sir Timothy Shelley that the Town Commissioners were willing to pay him 'One hundred and fifty pounds compensation for any loss or damage he may sustain.'[243] The next day 150 sovereigns were tendered to Sir Timothy Shelley, who refused them. The whole affair seems somewhat bizarre for Sir Timothy Shelley was a Town Commissioner and William Tribe, the Commissioners' Clerk negotiating the transaction, would appear to be one of the occupiers of the piece of land being acquired. As the parties had reached impasse the matter was referred to the Justices of the Peace so that the value of the land could be determined. At the Quarter Sessions meeting, held at the Sea House Hotel on the 26th April 1834, a jury assessed the value of the land to be £182.10s.0d.. This amount was invested in a Bank Annuities account, the $3^1/_2$% interest being taken annually by Sir Thomas Shelley.[244]

Prior to the site being purchased by the Town Commissioners it had been used by Dr. Rogers (who lived in South Place) as a garden, enclosed by an elder hedge.[245] The Town Commissioners were finally admitted to this piece of copyhold land at the Court Baron of Broadwater Manor held on the 1st June 1835. The Lord of the Manor, Mr. Harry Newland, in stark contrast to the actions of Sir Timothy Shelley, gratuitously enfranchised the land the next day, thus ensuring the Freehold status of the Town's first local government building.[246] Mr. Harry Newland took an important part in local affairs and owned a considerable amount of property in Worthing. He had become one of the Town Commissioners in 1807 and remained a member until they were superseded by the Local Board of Health in 1852. Henfrey Smail records

> 'At nearly all the meetings of the Commissioners he took the Chair, and in fact so invariably did he hold this office that on one of the rare occasions when he did not do so a footnote was added to the effect that "Mr. Harry Newland was not Chairman at this meeting"'.[247]

Work had already commenced on the construction of the Town Hall and after one or two delays, mainly connected with the clock, it was complete by the summer of 1835. The building was erected by a builder named Butler under the superintendence of Mr. Ralph Jones, who was the Town Surveyor at the time.[248] It has been suggested that the architect responsible for the design may have been Decimus Burton.[249] The two-storey building, in

Fig. 87 *Old Town Hall*

classical style with a portico and clock tower which housed the town clock, supplied by Mr. Vulliamy of London, cost £1215.8s.10d and was opened without ceremony in 1835.[250] It is remarkable that such an important event as the completion of the town's first civic building should have passed with so little notice. The Town Commissioners held their first meeting at the Town Hall on the 24th June 1835 when it was proposed by Mr. Dennett and seconded by Mr. Minshall that in future meetings of the Commissioners should be open to the public. This motion was carried and the first public meeting was held on the 23rd July 1835.[251]

In its early days there were cells below the Old Town Hall for the accommodation of prisoners. In *Glimpses of Old Worthing*, Edward Snewin and Henfrey Smail recall that the cells were

'so unsanitary that the smell arising from them often disturbed the deliberations of the Commissioners above. Here prisoners and vagrants were herded together indiscriminately, often suffering from various infectious fevers, which they spread from town to town.'[252]

Vagrants were given two pennyworth of bread each and lodgings under the Town Hall. So many of them came to the town, however, this was stopped and by 1860 strict measures for dealing with them eradicated the problem.[254]

At a special meeting of the Town Commissioners held on the 23rd July 1835 it was decided that one of the Beadles should live on the premises to keep it clean and, in addition to the prisoners, the hand operated fire-engine and ladder given to the town by Benjamin Haines Esq.[254] should be housed beneath the building.

By the twentieth century the prisoners and vagrants, together with the fire engine, had been replaced by public conveniences and an electric substation. Its large windows had also been blocked up in an attempt to keep out the ever-increasing traffic noise which had interfered with the deliberations within its walls.[255]

In 1837 Dr. Michael Morrah, whose eloquent address in 1818 raised the funds to build the Town Hall, presented to the town a large marble bust of George O'Brien, 3rd Earl of Egremont (1751-1837). He unfortunately died before paying for it. The sculptor, John Edward Carew (1785-1868), presented his bill firstly to the Town Commissioners and then to the doctor's executors, both of whom denied liability. In the end he had to make the best he could out of the financially embarrassing situation and presented the bust to the town himself, in the name of Dr. Morrah.[256] Kershaw's *Guide* of 1883 reveals that this marble bust was positioned on brackets in the main chamber between a landscape painting by 'Hobina' and another painting by a less eminent hand.[257]

Although the Old Town Hall was never considered an outstanding architectural example, it did represent the transitional style between the late Regency and early Victorian concept of a small public building and was for many years the architectural focal point for the main shopping streets. When it was finally demolished by Hall & Co. in early June 1966, at a cost of £1059 (only a few pounds less than it cost to build), enshrined in the building was over a century of Worthing's history. It had been erected at the end of Worthing's initial development into a 'Seaside Town', and those who both worked and governed the town from within its walls witnessed the struggle as the town accomplished the difficult transition to a Municipal Borough and a fast growing residential and holiday resort.

FOOTNOTES AND REFERENCES

Abbreviations used in the Footnotes / References

B.L.	British Library
B.W./P.R.	Broadwater Parish records deposited in the Worthing Town Hall Archives
Beauties of Eng. and Wales, Suss.	*The Beauties of England and Wales,* vol. xiv, by F. Shoberl [part 3], Sussex (1813)
Brandon, *Suss.Landscape*	P. Brandon, *The Sussex Landscape* (1974)
Brookfield, *Worthing*	H.C. Brookfield, *Worthing: a study of a modern coastal town* (1952)
Elleray, *Worthing*	D.R. Elleray, *Worthing ; A Pictorial History* (Phillimore 1977)
Elleray, *M.E.W.*	D.R. Elleray, *A Millennium Encyclopedia of Worthing History* (1998)
Evans, *Worthing* (1805, 1814)	J. Evans, *A Picture of Worthing* (1805; 2nd edn., 2 vols., Worthing 1814)
Farrant, *Georgian Brighton*	S. Farrant, *Georgian Brighton : 1740 -1820* University of Sussex Centre for Continuing Education 1980) Occ. Paper No. 13
Farrant, *Growth of Resorts*	S. Farrant, 'The Early Growth of the Seaside Resorts c.1750-1840' in *Sussex Environment, Landscape and Society* (Alan Sutton 1983)
Kerridge, *17th century Society & Economy*	R.G.P. Kerridge, 'Society and Economy along the Coastal plain during the seventeenth century', unpublished M.A. thesis - Humanities Dept. Brighton Polytechnic 1988.
Mackcoull's Worthing (1811)	*A Sketch of Worthing and its Environs,* printed for J. Mackcoull (1811)
Mackcoull's Worthing (1817)	*A Sketch of Worthing as it was and now is,* published by J. Mackcoull (1817)
P.R.O.	Public Record Office
Parry, *Suss. Coast*	J. D. Parry, *An Historical and Descriptive Account of the Coast of Sussex* (Brighton 1833)
S.A.C.	*Sussex Archaeological Collections* (1848 -)
S.N.Q.	*Sussex Notes and Queries* (1926 - 71)
SE to AD 1000	P Drewett, D. Rudling, and M. Gardiner, *The South East to AD 1000* (Longman 1988)
SE from AD 1000	P Brandon and B. Short, *The South East from AD 1000* (Longman 1988)
Shearsmith, *Worthing* (1824)	J. Shearsmith, *Topographical Description of Worthing* (Worthing, 1841)
Smail, *Beach House*	H. Smail, *Beach House* (Worthing 1948)
Smail, *Coaching Times*	H. Smail, *Coaching Times and After* (Worthing 1948)
Smail, *Map Story*	H. Smail , *The Worthing Map Story* (Worthing 1949)
Smail, *Warwick Ho.*	H. Smail, *Warwick House* (Worthing 1952)
Smail, *Worthing Road*	H. Smail, *The Worthing Road and its Coaches (Worthing 1943)*
Snewin and Smail, *Glimpses*	E. Snewin and H. Smail, *Glimpses of Old Worthing* (Worthing 1945)
Stafford's Worthing	*The New Worthing Guide,* printed for W. Stafford (Lewes,1810)
VCH	*Victoria History of the County of Sussex* Vol VI, Part 1, Bramber Rape (Southern part) ed. by T.P. Hudson (1980)
WB/TC/	Minutes of the meetings held by Worthing's Town Commissioners held in Worthing Borough Council's Archive.
W. R. L.	Worthing Reference Library
W.S.R.O.	West Sussex Record Office
Wallis's Worthing (1826)	*Wallis's Stranger in Worthing* (1826)
Walton, *Seaside*	J.K.Walton, *The English Seaside Resort: A Social History 1750 - 1914* (L.U.P. 1983)
Watering Places of G.B. and Fash Dir.	*Watering Places of Great Britain and Fashionable Directory* [1831-3]

1. EARLY SETTLEMENT

1.   *SE to AD 1000* p.2
2.   R. J. Devoy, 'Analysis of the geological evidence for Holocene sea-level movements in South East England'; *Proceedings of Geologists Association* (1982) Vol. 93
3.   *SE to AD 1000* p.2, 6 & 7
4.   R. J. Devoy, 'Analysis of the geological evidence for Holocene sea-level movements in South East England', *Proceedings of Geologists Association* (1982) Vol. 93
5.   A. Mawer and F.M. Stenton with J. E.B. Gover, *The Place Names of Sussex* English Place Name Society Vol VI pt.1 pp192 &193
6.   R.G.P. Kerridge, *A History of Lancing,* Phillimore (1979)
7.   A. Mawer and F.M. Stenton with J. E.B. Gover, *The Place Names of Sussex* English Place Name Society Vol VI pt.1 p. 192
8.   Report on a site investigation at Oakleigh Nursery, Dominion Way Worthing, carried out by Southern Testing Laboratories 1979.
9.   *SE to AD 1000* p.11
10. *Ibid.,* p. 24
11. R. Jessop, 'Britain's early Peoples' in *History of the English Speaking People* (Purnell) Vol 1 pp 28/29
12. *SE to AD 1000* pp 47 & 48
13. Curwin, *The Archaeology of Sussex* (London 1937) p.11
14. Col. A.H. Lane-Fox in 1867; E.H.Willett & P. Tindall in 1873-4
15. *SE to AD 1000* p. 50
16. V.C.H. p.67
17. Westm. Abbey Mun. 4072
18. *SE to AD 1000* pp. 127 & 129
19. J. R. Armstrong, *History of Sussex,* (Phillimore, third Edn. 1974) p32
20. *SE to AD 1000* p. 204
21. R. Legg, *Roman Britain* (1982), pp107/108 : Legg provides evidence to suggest that Britain became the 'granary of Europe'
22. *SE to AD 1000* p. 204
23. C. Taylor, *Fields in the English Landscape* (1982) p.48.
24. I. Margary, *Roman Centuriation at Ripe,* SAC Vol 81 (1940) pp.31/32. Margary indicates that the Roman measure was based on the *pes* or 'foot', shorter than the English foot and equivalent to 11.61 inches. Ten of these feet made one *pertica* or rod and 12 *pertica* an *actus.* This *actus* was thus 120 Roman feet in length. A rectangle measuring 120 by 240 Roman feet, or 2 square *actus,* was the area which it was considered, could be ploughed by a man with an ox in a day, hence it was termed a *jugerum* (jugerum = yoke)

25. C. Taylor, *Fields in the English Landscape* (1982) p.58
26. P. Brandon, *The Sussex Landscape* p. 58
27. I. Margary, *Roman Centuriation at Ripe,* SAC Vol 81 (1940) pp.31–41
28. H. C. Brookfield, *The Estuary of the Adur,* SAC Vol 90 (1952) p.160
29. When scaling off distances on the OS map and comparing them with the actual measurements, a maximum deviation was found of only about 47 feet [14.33m] over a distance of 11,605 feet [3,537.2m] which represents a 0.04% error. This was considered to be acceptable considering the intervening time span of some 1600 years, during which intensive ploughing, changes in field systems and re-development could be responsible for the minor shifts in the alignment of the ancient boundaries.
30. I. Margary, *The Chichester – Brighton Road,* SNQ Vol XI (1947) p.164
31. SAC Vol 65 (1924) pp. 263/264
32. SAC Vol 103 (1965) pp. 85/86
33. *Worthing Gazette ,* 13th May 1908
34. SAC Vol 98 (1960) p.25
35. SAC Vol 103 (1965) pp 84/85
36. SAC Vol 46 (1903) pp 155-162
37. M. Frost, *The Early History of Worthing* (1929) p.35
38. SNQ Vol 7 pp.234 –9
39. Louise Bashford *An Archaeological Watching Brief on Land off North Street / High Street, Worthing, West Sussex* (August 1996) SEAS Project No. 307
40. *SE to AD 1000* p. 246
41. R. Legg, *Romans in Britain* (1983) pp. 255/256
42. *SE to AD 1000* p.246
43. *Ibid.,* pp. 248 –251
44. The Patching hoard is now on permanent display in Worthing Museum.

2. MEDIEVAL WORTHING

1.   *SE to AD 1000* p.273
2.   S.W Woolridge and F. Goldring, *The Weald* (London 1972) pp. 195-196
3.   Archaeological Investigation (Stage 2) Summary Report - Homefield Annexe, Little High Street, Worthing. (Wessex Archaeology 1977)
4.   *SE to AD 1000* p.274 - Bishopstone in East Sussex is the most completely excavated site in South East England for the early

Anglo-Saxon period. In total 22 buildings were found, but a dense scatter of Anglo Saxon pottery extended beyond the excavated area and suggests that the overall settlement could have comprised up to c.60 buildings.
5.   P. V. Addyman and D. Leigh, 'The Anglo-Saxon Village at Charlton, Hampshire - second interim report. *Medieval Archaeology* Vol 17 pp 1-25
6.   Westm. Abbey Mun. 4072, 5469 f.25
7.   *SE to AD 1000* pp 292/293
8.   Westm. Abbey Mun. 4072, 5469 f25
9.   P. Brandon, *South Saxons* (Phillimore 1978) p.34
10. *SE to AD 1000* p.273
11. M. R. Standing, 'Regional Evolution: an evaluation of the emergence of contrasting regions in Medieval West Sussex.' Unpublished MA thesis, Humanities Dept. Brighton Polytechnic 1988.
12. M. Bell, 'Saxon Settlement and Buildings in Sussex' in P.Brandon (ed.) *The South Saxons* (Phillimore 1978) p. 52
13. J. McN. Dodgson, 'Place Names in Sussex: The material for a new look' in P. Brandon (ed.) *The South Saxons* (Phillimore 1978) pp. 57 -58
14. Using a computor based spreadsheet, the correlation between Saxon land ownership and the '-ingas' and '-ham' settlements was tested. All the '-ingas' holdings were either held by the King or had been granted by the Crown to Ecclesiastics. In the case of the '-hams' a more diffuse pattern of land ownership emerged, for in addition to the Royal household and Ecclesiastics many were also held by independent Saxon freeholders. *see* M.R. Standing 'Regional Evolution: an evaluation of the emergence of contrasting regions in Medieval West Sussex' Unpublished MA thesis, Humanities Dept. Brighton Polytechnic 1988
15. *SE to AD 1000* p.340.
16. *Ibid.;* D. Hey, *The Oxford Companion to Local History'* (B.C.A. 1966) p. 296
17. D. Hey, *The Oxford Companion to Local History'* (Oxford 1966) p. 43
18. M. Gardiner, 'Late Saxon Sussex c.650-1066' in *An Historical Atlas of Sussex* (ed.) K. Leslie and B. Short (Phillimore 1999) p.30
19. A. Mawer and F.M. Stenton with

J.E.B. Gover, 'The Place-Names of Sussex: Part 1' *E.P.N.S.* Vol vi pt.1 (C.U.P. 1986 reprint) p. xviii

20. S.N.Q. Vol 15 (1959) p. 134
21. I. Stewart, 'The Sussex Mints and their Moneyers', in *The South Saxons* (ed.) P. Brandon (Phillimore 1978) p. 90
22. S.N.Q. Vol 15 (1959) p. 134
23. *Ibid.*
24. J. J. North, *English Hammered Coinage Vol 1*, (1994) p.233
25. I. Stewart, 'The Sussex Mints and their Moneyers', in *The South Saxons* (ed.) P. Brandon (Phillimore 1978) pp 100/101.
26. *Domesday Book:Sussex* (General Editor) J. Morris (Phillimore 1976) 13.35 / 13.36
27. *The Domesday Book* (ed.) Thomas Hinde (Hutchinson 1985) p.340
28. M. Frost, *The Early History of Worthing* (Hove 1929) p.57
29. P. Morgan, *Domesday book and the Local Historian* (The Historical Association 1994) p.21
30. *Domesday Book:Sussex* (General Editor) J. Morris (Phillimore 1976) - Appendix
31. P.R.O - Census 1871
32. R. Welldon Finn, *Domesday Book : A Guide* (Phillimore 1986) p.54
33. Based on the Roman measurements given in I.D. Margery 'Roman Centuriation at Ripe' in SAC Vol 81 p.31 - Roman measurements were based on the *pes,* or foot, which was shorter than the English foot and equivalent to 11.61 inches. Ten *peches* made one *pertica,* or rod *and* 12 *perticae* made one *actus,* the measurement to which land areas were related. Each *actus* was thus 120 Roman feet or 116.05 English feet in length. The area of a 24 x 20 *actus* land parcel was, therefore 928.4 yards x 773.67 yards or 149 statute acres.
34. VCH Vol VI pt. 1 p.110 [Westm Abbey Mun 4072]
35. *The Domesday Book* (ed.) Thomas Hinde (Hutchinson 1985) p.340
36. J. R. Armstrong *History of Sussex* (Phillimore 3rd edition 1974) p.48
37. E. Cartwright, *Rape of Bramber* p.175
38. S. A. Moore, *History of the Foreshore and the law relating thereto,* (3rd edition London 1888) p.648
39. *Ibid.*, p.16
40. *Ibid.*, p.65
41. *Ibid.*, p.78
42. *Ibid.*, pp. 406 & 710
43. *Ibid.*, pp. 149 & 150
44. In Bramber Rape, Robert le Savage held the coastal plain holdings of Broadwater, Durrington, Worthing,

Sompting and Lancing together with the woodland holdings of Ashington, Buncton and Sedgewick and pasture at Angmering.

45. *Sussex Fines ii ,* SRS Vol 7 pp.62-3
46. VCH Sussex Vol VI pt. 1 p.69 [Complete Peerage ix. p.482]
47. R. Parker, *The Common Stream* (Paladin 1986 reprint) p.54
48. VCH Vol II [Rot Parl (Rec. Com.) i 147]
49. Westm. Abbey Mun. 5469 f.11; SAC Vol 5 p.236
50. W.S.R.O. - Worthing Court Books
51. *Chichester Chartulary* - SRS Vol XVI pp.170/1
52. VCH Sussex Vol II p.74 & 106
53. P.R.O. *Recovery Rolls* CP 43/911, rot 300; *Sussex Fines 1509-1833* SRS Vol XIX pp. 291-2; Tax Eccl. (Rec Com) 139.

3. THE AGRICULTURAL AND FISHING HAMLET

1. J. Richardson, *The Local Historian's Encyclopedia* (1975) p.40
2. VCH Vol VI pt. 1 p. 93
3. *Ibid.*, p. 119 & 120
4. *Ibid.*, p. 96
5. *Ibid.*, p. 67
6. Brookfield, *Worthing*
7. Snewin and Smail, *Glimpses* p.74
8. VCH Vol VI pt. 1 p. 92
9. Smail, *Map Story* p.65
10. Evans, *Worthing* (1805) p.38
11. Map drawn by Thomas Burdon - copy in Worthing Reference Library.
12. Snewin and Smail, *Glimpses* p.113
13. Evans, *Worthing* (1805) p.14
14. W.S.R.O. *Worthing Manorial Court Books*
15. R. Morgan, 'The History of Tanning in Chichester', *West Sussex History - Journal of the West Sussex Archives Society* (April 1992) No. 49, pp. 11-14
16. Close Rolls C54/3550 No. 22
17. W.S.R.O. - SAS - *Charles Stubbs Collection*
18. W.S.R.O. PHA 3263
19. VCH Vol VI pt. 1 p. 103
20. *Ibid.*, [Westm Abbey Mun. 4072; 5469 f.26]
21. R. D. Connor, *The Weights and Measures of England* (1987) p.36
22. *Ibid.*,
23. A. F. Nash ' Customary measure and open field strip size in Sussex', SAC Vol 121 (1983) pp. 112 & 113
24. A. F. Nash 'Perch and acre size in Medieval Sussex' SAC Vol. 116

(1978) p.61
25. The measured area of the open fields at Worthing was 313.91 statute acres and 459 customary acres. The derived ratio was, therefore, 313.91/459 = 0.68
26. *SE from 1000 AD* p.60
27. *Ibid.*, p.61
28. *Ibid.*, pp.62, 66 & 69
29. *Ibid.*, pp.93 & 94; VCH Vol VI Pt.1 p.109
30. VCH Vol VI pt. 1 p. 67 [E/ 79/189/42]
31. *Sussex Lay Subsidies* 1524-5 SRS Vol LVI pp.74-6
32. W.S.R.O Add ms 453, f2
33. Kerridge, *17th Century Society & Economy,* p.95
34. Joan Thirsk, 'Agricultural Regions and Agrarian History in England, 1500-1750' prepared for the *Economic History Society* (1987) p.28
35. Kerridge, *17th Century Society & Economy,* pp. 132-134
36. J. P. P. Horn 'The Distribution of Wealth in the Vale of Berkeley, Gloucestershire, 1660-1700,' *Southern History* Vol 3 (1981) p.82
37. L. Stone, 'Social mobility in England 1500-1700', *Past and Present* No. 33 p.21
38. Kerridge, *17th Century Society & Economy,* pp. 105, 106 & 139
39. SAC Vol 92 pp. 57 & 58
40. *The Agrarian History of England and Wales, Vol. V 1640-1756 ; Part 1 Regional Farming Systems* (ed.) Joan Thirsk (C.U.P. 1984) p.286
41. Kerridge, *17th Century Society & Economy,* pp. 28 - 30 & 189
42. W.R.S.O., Ep1/29/029/087
43. Kerridge, *17th Century Society & Economy,* p. 50
44. VCH Vol VI pt. 1 p. 76
45. J. H. Andrews, 'The Port of Chichester and the grain trade 1650-1750' SAC Vol 92 (1954) pp. 99 & 100
46. B. Breckon and J. Parker, *Tracing the History of Houses* (1996 reprint) p.19
47. R.W. Brunskill, *Illustrated Handbook of Vernacular Architecture* (1978) p.27
48. W.R.S.O. Ep1/29/029/033
49. W.R.S.O. Ep1/29/029/028
50. W.R.S.O. Ep1/29/029/096
51. M. W. Barley, *The English Farmhouse and Cottage* (London 1961) p.186
52. B. Breckon and J. Parker, *Tracing the History of Houses* (1996 reprint) p.22
53. 'The Hearth Tax, other later Stuart

tax lists and the Association Oath Rolls' compiled by J.S.W. Gibson, *Federation of Family History Societies* (1985) pp.4-7

54. Phillips map of Worthing published in Evans' *Picture of Worthing* (1814)

55. P. B. Park, 'My Ancestors were Manorial Tenants - How can I find out more about them?' *Society of Genealogists* (1990) Much of the general material on land tenure and the jurisdiction of the manorial courts has been summarised from this excellent booklet, which the interested reader should consult for all matters concerning the working of manorial courts and information on other manorial documents.

56. R.W. Brunskill, *Illustrated Handbook of Vernacular Architecture* (1978) p.22-24

57. B. Breckon and J. Parker, *Tracing the History of Houses* (1996 reprint) p.19

58. VCH Vol VI pt. 1 p. 109 [BL Add Ch 8893; Westm Abbey Mun. 5467 f.37; W.R.S.O.,Add MSS 453, ff 5v-6v, 461]

59. *Ibid.,* [Suss.Fines 1509-1833, ii (SRS Vol XX), p.367-8; C3/423/51; C142/518 no. 69]

60. W.B.C. Deeds A 83

61. VCH Vol VI pt. 1 p. 120

62. Calender of deeds in authors' collection

63. W.R.S.O. Ep1/29/029/110

64. Snewin and Smail, *Glimpses* p.145

65. Smail, *Map Story* p.97

66. *Mackcoull's Worthing* (1811) p.29

67. *Sussex Subsidies* (SRS Vol X p163; SRS LVI p.76

68. W.R.S.O. Ep1/29/029/025 & 062

69. *Protestation Returns* SRS Vol V pp. 37 - 39

70. PRO E179/258/14,17

71. Snewin and Smail, *Glimpses* p.142

72. W.S.R.O. Add MS 42996 - *Manor of Lancing Court Book, 1762-1910,* p.31

73. D. R. Elleray, *Worthing - Aspects of Change,* plate 146

74. Snewin and Smail, *Glimpses* p.41

75. *Ibid.,* pp. 33 & 143

76. *Ibid.,* p.18 ; Smail, *Map Story* p.74

77. Smail, *Map Story* pp.74/75

78. *Ibid.,* p.65

79. VCH Vol VI pt. 1 p. 109; *Worthing Survey* p 41; Snewin and Smail, *Glimpses* pp.146-7 and Smail, *Map Story* p.101

80. W.R.S.O. Ep1/29/029/015

81. Snewin and Smail, *Glimpses* p.41

82. *Ibid.,* pp. 33 & 143

83. *Worthing Herald,* 21st Sept. 1962

84. *Worthing Herald,* 28th July 1972

85. Snewin and Smail, *Glimpses* p.146

86. *Ibid.,*p.146

87. W.R.S.O. Ep1/29/029/068

88. W.R.S.O. Ep1/29/029/020

89. W.R.S.O. Ep1/29/029/016

90. W.R.S.O. Ep1/29/029/088

91. E. Heron-Allen, *Selsey Bill : Historic and Prehistoric* (London 1911) p.94

92. F. Harndon and J.S. North, *Old Brighton, Old Preston, Old Hove* (Brighton 1937) pp.26-29

93. VCH Vol VI pt. 1 pp. 47 & 93

94. W.S.R.O., *Vice Admiralty papers* EP1/55/26-240

95. W.R.S.O. Ep1/29/029/068

96. SAC Vol 35 pp. 98 & 99

97. C. Webb and A. E. Wilson, *Elizabethan Brighton - The Ancient Customs 1580* (Brighton 1952)

98. J. H. Farrant, 'The Rise and Decline of a South Coast Seafaring Town: Brighton 1550-1750', *The Mariners Mirror,* Vol. 71 No. 1 (1985) p.61

99. W.R.S.O. Ep1/29/029/020, 074 & 085; STC 1/18/E134 (MF184)

100. J. & S. Farrant, 'Brighton before Dr. Russell: An interim Report', *University of Sussex, Centre for continuing education,* occasional paper no.5 (Brighton 1976) p.25

101. W.R.S.O. Ep1/29/029/115

102. E. Heron-Allen, *Selsey Bill : Historic and Prehistoric* (London 1911) p.160

103. W.R.S.O. Ep1/29/029/095

104. A rental of the manor of Brighthemstone, survey made 30th August 1665 by Charles Goodwyn of Lewes, steward of the manor. Transcript deposited in Brighton Reference library.

105. W.R.S.O. Ep1/29/029/046

106. S. A. Moore, *History of the Foreshore and law relating thereto,* (London 1888) p.250

107. W.S.R.O. PHA 3263

108. VCH Vol VI pt. 1 p. 47

109. *Survey of the Coast of Sussex in the time of Queen Elizabeth* (ed.) M. A. Lower (Lewes 1870)

110. Rev. W. D. Parish, *A Dictionary of the Sussex Dialect* (1875) p.112; *The English Dialect Dictionary, Vol V, R-S,* (ed.) J. Wright, (reprint of 1970) pp. 7,15 & 719

111. SAC Vol 90, p. 155

112. VCH Vol VI pt. 1 p. 47

113. Charles Thomas-Stanford, 'An Abstract of the Court Rolls of the Manor of Preston (Preston Episcopi), S.R.S. Vol 27 (1921) pp. 19,21 & 41

114. VCH Vol VI pt. 1 p.92

115. W.R.S.O. Ep1/29/029/002

116. A rental of the manor of Brighthemstone, survey made

30th August 1665 by Charles Goodwyn of Lewes, steward of the manor. Transcript deposited in Brighton Reference library.

117. W.R.S.O. Ep1/29/029/016

118. T. W. Horsfield, *The History, Antiquities and Topography of the County of Sussex, Vol 1 (Lewes 1835)* p.124

119. VCH Vol VI pt. 1 p. 163

120. W.S.R.O., I/55/51

121. J. H. Farrant, 'The Rise and Decline of a South Coast Seafaring Town: Brighton 1550-1750', *The Mariners Mirror,* Vol. 71 No. 1 (1985) pp. 59 & 66

122. C. Fleet, *A Handbook of Brighton* (Brighton 1854) p.12

123. Rev. Canon J. H. Cooper, 'The Coverts part III,' SAC Vol 48 (1905) p.15

124. VCH Vol VI pt. 1 p. 113

125. Smail, *Map Story* p.59, Snewin and Smail, *Glimpses* p.24

126. VCH Vol VI pt. 1 p.113

127. VCH Vol VI pt. 1 p. 92

128. SAC Vol 35, pp. 98 & 99

129. Lord Ernle, *English Farming, Past and Present* (1919) pp.148 & 149.

4. THE GEORGIAN TOWN

1. J. A. R. Pimlot, *The Englishman's Holiday : A social history* (1947) pp. 50 & 51

2. Walton, *Seaside* p. 10

3. M. Blundell, *Blundell's Diary and Letter Book: 1702-28* (1952) pp.65-6

4. J. A. R. Pimlot, *The Englishman's Holiday : A social history* (1947) pp. 9-11

5. Walton, *Seaside* p. 10

6. Evans, *Worthing* (1814) p.64

7. Universal British Dictionary, iv (1798) p.580

8. Dallaway and Cartwright, *History of West Sussex* 33n

9. *Topographer* iv, (1791)

10. Smail, *Map Story* p.65

11. Smail, *Warwick Ho.* pp.9-11

12. Farrant, *Growth of Resort*s p.208

13. Evans, *Worthing* (1805) p.17

14. W.S.R.O., Land Tax (1786-88)

15. *Ibid.,* (1789) - property now shown as three times its rateable value for the previous year.

16. *Ibid.,* (1789-90)

17. Evans, *Worthing* (1805) p.35

18. SAC Vol 23 p. 223

19. *Topographer* iv, (1791) p.149

20. W.S.R.O. Add Mss 27808

21. H. Smail, 'A Princess comes to Town' in *Worthing Parade No.1* (Worthing 1951) p.15; Snewin and Smail, *Glimpses* p.64

22. Farrant, *Georgian Brighton* p.3
23. W.S.R.O. Add MSS 27808
24. *Sussex Weekly Advertiser,* 10th March 1794
25. W.S.R.O., Land Tax (1795)
26. *Sussex Weekly Advertiser,* 10th March 1794
27. W.S.R.O., Land Tax (1793)
28. Elleray *M.E.W.* p.142
29. From Abstract of Title in the possession of the authors.
30. W.S.R.O., Land Tax (1797)
31. Smail, *Map Story* p.93; Snewin and Smail, *Glimpses* p.80
32. Walton, *Seaside* p. 82
33. VCH Vol VI pt. 1 p. 93 [later correspondence of Geo III (ed.) A. Aspinall, iii pp. 92-3]
34. H. Smail, 'A Princess comes to Town' in *Worthing Parade No.1* (Worthing 1951) p.15
35. Walton, *Seaside* p. 218
36. *The Times,* 8th September 1802
37. Brookfield, *Worthing*
38. Smail, *Worthing Road,* p.95
39. *Ibid.,* p.95
40. Smail, *Map Story* p.95
41. Smail, *Worthing Road,* p.95
42. P.R.O. : Census 1801, 1811
43. *The Times,* 31st August 1802
44. W.S.R.O. Add Mss 460-1
45. H. G. Hunt, 'Land Tax Assessments' *The Historical Association Short Guide No. 16* p.86 - In 1798 Land Tax was fixed at four shillings in the pound and made a permanent charge on land and proprietors were given the option to redeem at fifteen years purchase.
46. Snewin and Smail, *Glimpses* p.36
47. Information derived from 'Abstract of Title' in authors' possession.
48. Snewin and Smail, *Glimpses* p.56
49. Evans, *Worthing* (1805) p.13
50. *Ibid.,* pp.16-18
51. *Ibid.,* pp.16-17
52. Snewin and Smail, *Glimpses* p.56; D. R. Elleray, *Worthing : Aspects of Change* p. 143
53. Farrant, *Georgian Brighton* p.20
54. Snewin and Smail, *Glimpses* p.36; Smail, *Map Story* p.88
55. Evans, *Worthing* (1805) p.21
56. *Ibid.,* p. 33
57. Farrant, *Growth of Resort*s p.211
58. Farrant, *Georgian Brighton* p.4
59. Walton, *Seaside* p. 191
60. *The Times,* 6th August 1798
61. Snewin and Smail, *Glimpses* p.64
62. Evans, *Worthing* (1805) p.19
63. Shearsmith, *Worthing* (1841) p.46-9; M. Odell, *More About the Old Theatre Worthing* (1945) pp. 38-44
64. Elleray *M.E.W.* p.38
65. W.S.R.O. Ep1/29 Broadwater 138
66. Evans, *Worthing* (1805) p.22; *Beauties of Eng. and Wales, Suss.* p.104

67. Evans, *Worthing* (1805) p.18
68. J. Anderson and E. Swinglehurst, *The Victorian and Edwardian Seaside* (1978) pp. 70/71.
69. H. Smail, 'A Princess comes to Town' in *Worthing Parade No.1*(Worthing 1951) p.9
70. *Grand Tour to Worthing* (1805) pp. 71-80
71. WBC/TC/2 p.405
72. Walton, *Seaside* p. 159
73. Smail, *Map Story* p.65
74. Farrant, *Georgian Brighton* p.4
75. *Worthing Gazette,* 18th March 1975
76. WBC : Deeds A6
77. Walton, *Seaside* p. 159
78. J. Austen, *Lady Susan: The Watsons: Sanditon,* (ed) M. Drabble (1976)
79. Evans, *Worthing* (1805) p.15
80. Ibid., p.16; Snewin and Smail, *Glimpses* p.119; *Worthing Gazette,* 12th March 1975
81. *Worthing Gazette,* 12th March 1975
82. Smail, *Map Story* p.88
83. WB/TC/1 pp. 244/245
84. M. T. Odell, *The Old Theatre Worthing 1807-1855* (Worthing 1938) pp.12/13
85. W.R.L. 'Sussex Collection - Press Cuttings' 1870
86. WBC : Deeds A 570
87. Farrant, *Georgian Brighton* p.26
88. M. T. Odell, *The Old Theatre Worthing 1807-1855* (Worthing 1938) pp.14-17
89. Smail, *Warwick Ho.* p. 27
90. WBC : Deeds A570
91. Snewin and Smail, *Glimpses* p.36
92. *Ibid.,* p116
93. *Mackcoull's Worthing* (1811) p.20
94. *Stafford's Worthing* p.2
95. Snewin and Smail, *Glimpses* p.116
96. *Stafford's Worthing* p.9
97. Smail, *Map Story* p.87
98. Walton, *Seaside* p. 158
99. *The Times,* 8th September 1802
100. Farrant, *Growth of Resorts* p.216
101. Town Act 43, Geo III, c.59 (Local & Personal)
102. Snewin and Smail, *Glimpses* p.43
103. Town Act 43, Geo III, c.59 (Local & Personal)
104. VCH Vol VI pt. 1 p. 115
105. VCH Suss. Vol 2 p.218 - 1801 Census
106. WB/TC/1 p. 3 & 4
107. Smail, *Coaching Times,* p.136-7
108. Evans, *Worthing* (1805) p.32; Smail, *Map Story* p.73-5 & 102-7

109. Evans, *Worthing* (1805) p.17
110. see Phillip's map of Worthing 1814 - reproduced as Fig. 75 originally published in the second edition of John Evans' *Picture of Worthing* (1814)
111. WBC : Deeds A 405
112. WB/TC/1 p.54
113. Smail, *Map Story* p.102
114. *The Times,* 31st August 1802: 20th September 1806; *Stafford's Worthing* p.8-10
115. Parry, *Suss. Coast,* p.353
116. BW/1818 Surveyors Rate Book
117. Snewin and Smail, *Glimpses* p.124
118. *Mackcoull's Worthing* (1811) pp.64/65
119. Snewin and Smail, *Glimpses* p.125
120. Evans, *Worthing* (1805) p.19
121. Snewin and Smail, *Glimpses* p.134
122. *Stafford's Worthing* p.9
123. Smail, *Map Story* p.88
124. Evans, *Worthing* (1805) p.17
125. *Stafford's Worthing; Evans, Worthing (1815)*
126. Evans, *Worthing* (1805) pp.29/30
127. WBC/CEB 1821 - An unoccupied portion of modern No. 34 Warwick Street is described as the 'Old Bank'.
128. P. R. Jenkins, *Sussex Money,* (Pulborough 1987) pp. 14 & 15
129. *Ibid.,* p.16
130. *Mackcoull's Worthing* (1811) p. 18
131. Snewin and Smail, *Glimpses* p.127
132. *Ibid.*
133. P. R. Jenkins, *Sussex Money,* (Pulborough 1987) pp. 36 & 40
134. Snewin and Smail, *Glimpses* p.126
135. P. R. Jenkins, *History of Banking in Sussex* (1986) pp. 11, 12 & 26
136. WBC : Deeds A 405
137. Snewin and Smail, *Glimpses* p.134; Smail, *Coaching Times,* p. 83
138. W.S.R.O *Land Tax 1808 - 1814*
139. *Universal Dictionary* (Readers Digest 1992) p.973
140. WBC/TC/1 p.100
141. Snewin and Smail, *Glimpses* p.133
142. WBC: Deeds A.400
143. Snewin and Smail, *Glimpses* p.133
144. WBC : Deeds A 400
145. WBC: Deeds A 416
146. Snewin and Smail, *Glimpses* p.133
147. WBC: Deeds A 429/2
148. Snewin and Smail, *Glimpses* p.130

149. WBC: Deeds A 429/2
150. *Ibid.,*
151. WBC/TC/1 pp. 30 & 40
152. Worthing Town & Market Act 49 Geo III, c.114 (Local & Personal) p.6
153. *Ibid.*
154. WB/TC/1 p.47
155. Evans, *Worthing* (1814) p.57; *Mackcoull's Worthing* (1811) p.26
156. WBC/TC/1 p.52
157. Worthing Town & Market Act 49 Geo III, c.114 (Local & Personal) p.2
158. WBC: Deeds A 570
159. WBC/TC/1 p.54
160. *Ibid.*, p.59
161. Snewin and Smail, *Glimpses* p.130; *Beauties of Eng. and Wales,* Suss. p.104
162. WBC/TC/1 p.63
163. *Ibid.,*
164. WBC/TC/1 pp. 174 & 175
165. *Ibid.,* pp. 78 & 79
166. Snewin and Smail, *Glimpses* pp.130 & 131
167. WBC/TC/1 pp. 201 & 202
168. *Ibid.,* p. 237
169. *Ibid.,* p.82
170. *Ibid.,* pp. 78 & 79
171. *Ibid.,* pp. 76 & 77
172. *Ibid.,* pp. 214 - 217
173. *Ibid.,* p. 217
174. Snewin and Smail, *Glimpses* p.132
175. Brookfield, *Worthing*
176. PRO - MRL 21(2)
177. Inclosure Act, 45 Geo III, C.70 (1805)
178. B. Short, 'The Changing Rural Society and Economy in Sussex 1750-1945' in *Sussx, Environment, Landscape and Society* (Alan Sutton 1983) p.148
179. *Beauties of Eng. and Wales,* Suss. p.104
180. Smail, *Map Story* p.109; PRO Census 1811, 1821.
181. Deeds loaned to the authors for the research for this book.
182. Parry, *Suss. Coast,* p.354; *Mackcoull's Worthing* (1811) p.12
183. Smail, *Warwick Ho.,* p.19
184. Elleray, *M.E.W.* p. 36
185. Smail, *Map Story* p.93
186. *Wallis's Worthing* (1826) pp. 14 & 15
187. W.R.S.O. Add ms 468
188. *Mackcoull's Worthing* (1811) p.67
189. Elleray, *M.E.W.* p. 135
190. For those wishing to know more about the Chapel of Ease - see D. R. Elleray *St. Pauls Church : A History and Description* (Optimus Books 1999)
191. J. Shearsmith, *Topographical Description of Worthing* (Worthing 1824)

192. W.S.R.O. Ep. 1/17/44, ff. 95v-97v.
193. *Mackcoull's Worthing* (1811) pp. 139-42
194. *Mackcoull's Worthing* (1817) pp.32 & 33
195. Elleray, *M.E.W.* p. 120
196. WBC/TC/1 p.163
197. *Ibid.,* pp. 42,163 & 175
198. *Ibid.,* p.163
199. *Ibid.,* p.175
200. *Ibid.,* p.183
201. *Ibid.,* p.190
202. Smail, *Warwick Ho.* pp.39-58
203. *Ibid.,* p. 46 & 51
204. Univ. Brit Dict. iv (1798) p.580
205. Pigot Nat. Dir (1823-4) 524; *Ibid.,* (1828-9) pp. 727 & 728
206. Smail, *Beach House,* pp. 10 & 11
207. *Wallis's Worthing* (1826) : plan
208. Snewin and Smail, *Glimpses* p.77
209. Town Planning Review xxiii, p. 151
210. P. Holden, *Typhoid, Bombs and Matron: The History of Worthing Hospital* (Worthing Hospital League of Friends)
211. *Worthing a Survey of Times, Past and Present* (ed. F. W. Migeod (Worthing 1938) pp. 171/172
212. Smail, *Map Story* p.109; Elleray *M.E.W.* p.144
213. Snewin and Smail, *Glimpses* p.61
214. Ibid.; Elleray *M.E.W.* p.89
215. *Watering Places of G.B. and Fash Dir.,* p. 16 ; *Elleray, M.E.W.* p. 95
216. Snewin and Smail, *Glimpses* pp. 77 & 80; *Brighton Gazette,* 15th July 1835
217. Parry, *Suss. Coast,* p.357
218. Snewin and Smail, *Glimpses* p. 86
219. *Ibid.,* p.87
220. Elleray *M.E.W..* p.109
221. *Wallis's Worthing* (1826) p. 6-7, 21-2.
222. Smail, *Warwick Ho,.* p. 11
223. Farrant, *Growth of Resorts,* p.218
224. M. Odell, *The Old Theatre, Worthing* (1938) p. 78
225. Town Planning Rev. xxiii, p. 151
226. WBC/TC/1 p. 260 & 261
227. Worthing Town & Market Act. 49, Geo iii, c114 (Local & Personal)
228. WBC/TC/1 pp. 266 & 267
229. *Ibid.,* pp. 21 & 23
230. Worthing Town and Market Act 1 & 2, Geo IV, c. 59 (Local & Personal)
231. WBC/TC/2 pp. 51 & 52
232. Snewin and Smail, *Glimpses* p.43
233. Evans, *Worthing* (1805) p.32 & 33
234. WBC/TC/2 p.275
235. *Ibid.,* pp. 391, 392 & 395
236. BW/PR/A Assessment Committee

meeting 20th October 1837
237. Ibid., Assessment Committee meeting 1st December 1837
238. Smail, *Map Story,* p.123
239. WBC/TC/2 pp. 100, 104 & 167
240. Smail, *Map Story,* p.123
241. Worthing Town and Market Act 1 & 2, Geo IV, c. 59 (Local & Personal)
242. WBC/TC/2 p.242
243. WBC: Deeds A 236/8
244. Master of the Rolls: Westminster: B 1833 fo. 1030
245. Snewin and Smail, *Glimpses* p.98
246. WBC: Deeds A 236/8
247. H. Smail, *Offington, Broadwater Manor, Charmandean* (Worthing, 1950) p.70
248. Snewin and Smail, *Glimpses* p.98
249. Elleray, *Worthing,* notes to plate 29
250. V.C.H. Vol VI pt.1, p.117
251. Smail, *Map Story,* p.123
252. Snewin and Smail, *Glimpses* p.98
253. *Worthing Herald,* 6th June 1966
254. WBC/TC/1 p.166
255. *Worthing Herald,* 6th June 1966
256. *West Sussex Gazette,* 21st July 1966
257. G. D. S. Kershaw, *Guide and Handbook to Worthing and its Vicinity* (1883), pp. 13 & 14

INDEX